MIND

Shows how latest scientific discoveries can help you develop
the personal PK power to move large objects with
your mind.

MINDREACH

by

J. H. BRENNAN

THE AQUARIAN PRESS
Wellingborough, Northamptonshire

First published 1985

© J. H. BRENNAN 1985

British Library Cataloguing in Publication Data

Brennan, J. H.
  Mindreach.
  1. Psychokinesis
  I. Title
  133.8'8   BF1371

  ISBN 0-85030-386-9

*The Aquarian Press is part of the
Thorsons Publishing Group*

Printed and bound in Great Britain

Contents

Acknowledgements

I first heard of the Batcheldor technique from my friend and colleague Tim Fynes-Smith, who has spent many years investigating poltergeist and allied phenomena. Initially, I paid little attention since it seemed that Batcheldor and his group were engaged on little more than a revival of Victorian table-turning — a fashionable parlour game in its heyday.

But this snap judgement proved entirely superficial and once I began to study the published and private records of Batcheldor's experiments, I realized with mounting excitement that something of a breakthrough had been taking place, virtually unnoticed, in the field of serious psychical research.

This book is an attempt to bring the Batcheldor methodology before the wider public it deserves; and to encourage other groups to put the techniques into practice. The work would have been impossible without the generous co-operation of Tim Fynes-Smith, who turned over to me his entire files not only on Batcheldor but on his extensive poltergeist investigations as well.

I am also deeply indebted to Kenneth Batcheldor himself who, despite the pressures of his own affairs, took time to answer my questions, examine and comment on the finished manuscript and freely permitted me to quote from his own extensive papers.

On this latter point, however, I had better state clearly that the responsibility for any shortcomings in the book you are about to read is entirely my own.

1
Strange Things

Strange things happen to unlikely people.

A research student, visiting my home just the other day, noticed some of my earlier books on the paranormal and was encouraged to ask my advice. She had moved some years ago into a small terraced house, part of which had recently been extended. Since that time, she had been quite unable to live in the original portion of the house (which was more than 150 years old). When she tried to remain in these rooms for any length of time, she became unaccountably upset to the point of panic. Often she found herself actually running into the newer extension 'for safety'. She suspected a haunting, although she saw no ghostly figures nor heard any ghostly sounds. She made enquiries in the neighbourhood and found the previous tenant, an old woman, had been 'unhappy'. Apart from that, there did not seem to be any dramatic history associated with the house. Nonetheless, she could not stem her panic while she was in the older section and did not know what to do.

Only a few months previously, an elderly friend of mine had undergone an even more disturbing experience. Confined to bed following a heart attack, she was disturbed by a midnight visitation by an entity of some sort. The creature, which she could sense but not actually see, gradually approached her bed, then struck her a resounding blow on the solar plexus, causing her considerable pain.

Although reluctant to tell her family, the woman felt that it would be dangerous to remain where she was since any repetition of the attack might adversely affect her recovery. Fortunately the family proved sympathetic if a little incredulous and her bed was duly moved. Her daughter, a middle-aged woman, and her granddaughter, a teenager, moved into the bedroom. After an uneventful few days, both the woman and the girl were awakened at 4 a.m. by the invisible intruder, which attempted to strangle the daughter who, however, eventually fought it off successfully.

My friend associated these frightening manifestations with a poltergeist which had troubled the house two years previously. The noisy ghost had caused raps, produced the stench of drains and eventually begun to smash ornaments before she drove it away 'with prayer'.

Five years ago, a successful Dublin barrister who was entertaining a friend and myself in his home, called me quietly away from the dinner table and asked me to come upstairs where he had something to show me. We went up to a room which featured a small hanging mobile — a popular type of ornamentation which is comprised of various light metallic shapes hung from slim wires. Wind currents will normally keep mobiles in motion, but with doors and windows closed, this one hung still.

'Watch this,' said the barrister, and pointed his forefinger at one of the shapes. After a moment, it began to spin wildly. He then went on to demonstrate that he could do the same thing to any of the shapes and permitted me to examine both the mobile and himself to satisfy myself there was no trickery involved.

It transpired he did not have to point to make a shape move. All he required was to concentrate on it deeply. The pointing was simply to demonstrate which shape he was concentrating on. He had, he said, discovered his curious ability quite by chance while lying in bed. It was confined to the movement of small, light objects, suspended so that they could be easily influenced. He did not intend to develop the talent since it frightened his wife.

Diverse though they appear, I believe all three of these cases have a common denominator: and that the third is the key to them all. In a sense, this whole book is an attempt to justify that belief; but it is something more as well. In recent years, there have been certain fascinating, yet little reported, developments in the realm of scientific research into the paranormal, which suggest that perfectly ordinary people may train themselves to produce phenomena which were once thought of as occult, miraculous or psychic. Clear descriptions of the techniques involved are given later in the book, so that you, the reader, may have an opportunity to test them for yourself.

I am not an academic and have never developed the academic's literary style, so that technical terms will be kept to a minimum throughout. The two most commonly used are worth a short, but careful, definition here. The first is 'psychokinesis', generally shortened to PK.

Psychokinesis is the term coined by psychical researchers to describe a process by which material objects are apparently influenced directly by the human mind. The word *apparently* is important here. In a typical demonstration of PK, the experimenter will, like the Dublin barrister, concentrate on a target object; and if the demonstration proves successful, the object moves. To both experimenter and observers, this looks very much like mind moving matter, but the situation may not be quite so simple as that.

Newtonian physics attributes a quality called *inertia* to any object in its resting state. The overcoming of *inertia* requires energy input and the mathematical laws which govern the amount of energy required for any given mass of object are very well known. The human brain does indeed generate a measurable degree of electrical energy, but in far too small a quantity to influence external objects. Since we know that energy *must* be involved somewhere in the PK process, we need to know where it is coming from. If it does not come from the brain, then it may, perhaps, come from the body. Alternatively, some external energy source may be used. In either case, we are dealing with a *type* of energy more or less unsuspected by the mainstream of modern psychics. Furthermore, this energy — whatever it may be and wherever it originates — can obviously be *directed* by the human mind.

Thus, unless we are prepared yet again to rewrite laws of physics which have stood the test of generations, we have to consider the popular 'mind over matter' concept as inaccurate. In PK phenomena, we are really discussing the mental directing of some largely unknown type of energy originating from an unknown source. The two 'unknowns' make this a frustrating picture to contemplate, but it is the best we can do for now.

The second technical term is 'poltergeist', which, certainly on the face of it, does not seem to have very much to do with PK. *Poltergeist* is a term taken directly from the German: *geist* means ghost and *polter* means noise – hence 'noisy ghost'. It is a graphic description. Through the centuries, poltergeist phenomena have so successfully mimicked violent hauntings that most lay people – and a substantial number of specialists – never stop to consider that poltergeists may not be all they seem.

This is an important point and one which provides the initial springboard of our present investigation. The entire introductory section of this book is concerned with the poltergeist in a representative cross-section of its many forms. If the case histories presented seem a little divorced from the central thesis of a book which purports to investigate the latent abilities of your mind and mine, then please be patient. The linkage will, I hope, become obvious at a later stage.

2
The Noisy Ghost

Pliny the Younger was a Roman orator who lived during the first century AD. Among his surviving papers is a letter describing something very odd which happened in a house in Athens.

According to Pliny, the building lay idle for some years and was actually falling into disrepair when it attracted the attention of a philosopher named Athenodorus.

Philosophers were not, apparently, very well paid in those days, for what chiefly interested Athenodorus was the possibility of a cheap rental. He approached the owners and discovered that he could have it for a pittance. The problem, they told him openly, was that the house was haunted.

Athenodorus took the news philosophically and moved in. It is possible he did not believe in ghosts, for the ancients were by no mean universally superstitious. In any case, he settled down to work on the first evening in his new residence and quickly forgot all about the haunting — until, that is, he heard the rattling of chains . . .

The philosopher looked up from his manuscript to find himself staring at the beckoning figure of an old man, fettered and chained. With considerable aplomb, Athenodorus returned to his work. But the noise of the chains proved impossible to ignore so that eventually he was forced to get up and follow the apparition outside.

He was led into the garden where the ghost abruptly vanished in the middle of a shrub setting. Thoroughly intrigued by now, Athenodorus dug on the spot and subsequently discovered skeletal human remains, wrists and ankles still encased by fetters.

In writing the account, Pliny remarks that when the remains were reburied with proper ceremony, the haunting ceased. Whatever else one may say about this, or indeed the appearance of the apparition itself, the rattling of the chains allows us to place this manifestation in the realm of the poltergeist, or 'noisy ghost' — one of the first such case studies ever to go on written record. But it was not the last.

Any author who attempts to study poltergeists suffers from an embarrassment of source material. Even minimum research leaves the impression that poltergeists have swept through history like an epidemic. The impression is, of course, subjective — at any given time in any given place, poltergeist phenomena are rare enough. But the sheer collective volume of case histories is so enormous that the writer's task becomes one of selection rather than discovery — which is all by way of saying that however many cases we investigate here, the result will never be exhaustive.

If Pliny's poltergeist slides into our specialized history by reason of the noise it made, another early case study is far more typical of poltergeist phenomena in general.

This one occurred in a farmhouse on the Rhine towards the end of the ninth century AD when, according to the *Annales Fuldenses* an 'evil spirit' made its presence felt by throwing stones.

The manifestation quickly progressed to the banging of walls with such violence that they actually shook, then to the burning of the farmer's crops as soon as they were harvested. As if this were not trouble enough, the ghost developed a voice and was soon accusing the farmer of adultery.

Word of the haunting began to spread and eventually reached the ears of the Bishop of Mainz who despatched priests armed with relics and holy water to exorcise the spirit. Regrettably the poltergeist proved no respecter of the cloth and when the priests began their sprinkling and hymn singing, it replied with a volley of stones.

The extant accounts do not say who won the battle, nor what happened to the ghost. Modern case studies, which are generally better documented and more conclusive, would suggest that the exorcism failed (since exorcism usually does against poltergeists) and that the 'ghost', after making a thorough nuisance of itself for several weeks or months, simply faded away.

Exorcism is certainly known to have failed in the case described by Gerald of Wales who lived from 1174 to 1223. This noisy ghost flung mud, cut holes in clothing and 'conversed with men' in an aggressive and derisory manner. Priests who arrived to send off the imp were treated exactly as if they had been laymen — a development which led Gerald to conclude that while exorcism might be effective against 'true demons' it did not appear to prevail against mischievous entities like the mud-slinger. He suspected that the 'ghost' was probably no more than a nature spirit.

Gerald was one of the first to speculate on the actual nature of the poltergeist and if his ideas may seem a little simplistic to us now, his stance was a notable step forward. The phenomenon itself continued to march across the pages of history with written accounts becoming progressively fuller and more detailed.

The early years of the sixteenth century (1524, to be exact) saw the emergence of a case interesting for its similarities with what later came to be known as Spiritualist phenomena.

Anthoinette de Grolée, an 18-year-old nun in the Convent of St Pierre in Lyons woke one night with the impression that someone had just kissed her, then made the sign of the cross. As she sat up, she heard rapping noises, apparently from under the floor. It soon became obvious that these noises had no natural origin and before long the convent was jammed with interested observers.

Someone suggested that communication be established and a code was worked out. Through the code, the raps claimed to be the spirit of a second nun, Alix de Telieux, who had fled from the convent after stealing some jewels, and subsequently died in misery.

The body of Alix was brought back to the convent and given a decent burial. But unlike the case described by Pliny, this charitable act failed to stop the haunting. The King's Almoner,

Adrien de Montalembert, described how the ghost was able to give answers 'known to no mortal' and — of far more interest in our present context — how the entity managed to make Sister Anthoinette levitate high into the air.

Those of strong religious conviction seem to have been a particular focus of poltergeist activity in times gone by. Less than a hundred years after the convent case, a Huguenot Minister, Francois Perrault, was plunged into a supernatural nightmare when he returned to his parish at Macon in September 1612 after a brief leave of absence. He reached his home to be greeted by his terrified wife and maidservant, who could scarcely wait to tell him the incredible story of what had been happening to them.

What had been happening to them was indeed incredible: curtains had been drawn in the night, bedclothes pulled off by invisible hands, ornaments and small furnishings had been thrown around in empty rooms. Night after night, the house resounded to loud crashes and bangs.

If the Reverend M. Perrault was at all sceptical, it did not last long. On the night of his return, the poltergeist obligingly threw pots around the kitchen. A week later, the ghost began to whistle, then call out 'Minister' in a shrill voice, and finally to sing a simple song.

Like so many other poltergeist sites, the Minister's home soon became the focus of popular attention and before long the ghost was conversing volubly with various visitors and taking every opportunity to spread malicious (and generally inaccurate) gossip about the townspeople. The violence of the manifestation increased until stones weighing two and three pounds each were being thrown around the house. The curious fact that little real damage was caused led M. Perrault to conclude that his home was under God's personal protection.

Whatever one thinks about this, there are indications that the Perrault poltergeist was a helpful enough entity in its own odd way. The maidservant managed to strike up a friendly relationship with it — to such a degree that it would imitate her accent and, when requested, bring her wood.

Not all such spirits were so benevolent. Richard Bovet's *Account of the Daemon of Spraiton in the County of Devon* gives the flavour of malevolence so strongly that I cannot resist quoting directly from the original despite the difficulties modern readers may have with the style.

The *Account* reads in part:

> One time the young mans head was thrust into a very strait place, betwixt a Beds head and a Wall, and forced by the strength of divers men to be removed thence, and that not without being much hurt, and bruised so that much blood appeared about it. . . . At divers other times he hath been in danger to be strangled with Cravats and Handkerchiefs that he hath worn about his Neck, which have been drawn so close that with the sudden violence he hath near been choaked and hardly escaped death. . . . At another time one of his Shoe-strings was observed (without the assistance of any hand) to come of its own accord out of his shoe and fling itself to the other side of the Room; the other was crawling after it, but a Maid espying that, with her hand drew it out, and it strangely clasp'd and curl'd about her hand like a living Eel.

The Spraiton 'daemon' put in its appearance towards the end of the seventeenth century. The eighteenth opened in equally fine style with a poltergeist plaguing another clergyman. This time the victim was the Revd Samuel Wesley (whose grandson, John, would later found the Methodist Church).

At first, the Revd Wesley was unaware that anything untoward was going on, despite the fact that his maidservant had heard loud groans in the dining room and other members of the household were subjected to raps and knocks originating from the nursery. When the family eventually decided to tell him, he did not believe them, but that night loud knocks by his bedside persuaded him completely.

The haunting worsened. The house was filled with footsteps, crashing noises and a sound like someone planing wood. Mrs Wesley discovered an animal 'like a badger' under a bed in the nursery. There is some doubt as to whether it was a real badger:

a manservant, who saw it in the dining room, claimed it was a white rabbit.

These Alice in Wonderland activities continued for two months during the early winter of 1716, then stopped as inexplicably as they had begun. The Wesley family put the occurrences down to witchcraft, against which the Revd Samuel had often preached.

The mid eighteenth century saw the appearance of one of the most famous poltergeists in history — the Cock Lane Ghost. This entity first attracted attention by producing knocks in the home of Richard Parsons, who was Clerk of St Sepulchre's Church in London. These were followed by scratching noises behind the wainscoting.

Parsons himself thought the cause might be his next-door neighbour, a cobbler by trade. Later he seems to have concluded it was mice or rats, since he called in a carpenter to remove the wainscoting. Despite this sensible move and, presumably, protests to the cobbler, the raps grew louder.

Word of the manifestation began to spread. A local publican claimed he saw a ghostly figure in white at the house about a month after the first noises began. Parsons called on the assistance of an ecclesiastical friend, the Revd John Moore of St Sepulchre's. Moore decided to establish communication and worked out a simple rap code.

At this point the story took a dramatic turn. The ghost claimed to be the spirit of a woman named Fanny Lynes, returned from the dead in order to point an accusing finger at her lover, William Kent. Kent, she said, had killed her by putting red arsenic in her beer.

Both Kent and Lynes, living ostensibly as husband and wife, had been tenant lodgers in Parson's house until Fanny contracted smallpox. Kent moved with her to another house, but the disease killed her in February, 1760.

That the ghost actually *was* Fanny Lynes is highly unlikely, since she was still alive — and indeed still living in Parson's house — when the first raps were heard. But a good story is a good story and this one found a wide public. Parsons himself certainly chose to believe it, probably because he disliked Kent, to whom he owed money.

Poltergeists are good copy, as anyone who reads the Sunday newspapers will readily agree. They were equally good copy in the eighteenth century, especially when a juicy murder scandal was attached. The *Public Leader* carried an account of the man who had brought a young woman from Norfolk in order to poison her in London. Kent, who had previously been aware of the slur on his name, happened to read the piece and went off to the Revd Moore for advice.

By now Moore — and many others — had become convinced the spirit manifested with the help of Parsons' 10-year-old daughter, Elizabeth. He suggested that Kent should attend a seance. Kent agreed and in the child's bedroom listened in horror while the raps accused him of murder. 'Thou art a lying spirit!' he screamed.

This sort of human drama is what entertainment is all about. Cock Lane became the most notorious street in London. Day after day it was crowded with carriages and pedestrians as the curious hoped to catch a glimpse of a ghost — or at very least of an accused murderer. Inevitably some took the whole thing more seriously than others. A sort of psychical investigation committee, which included the famous Dr Johnson, examined 10-year-old Elizabeth and, when she failed to produce raps to order, concluded the whole case was fraudulent.

Nonetheless, the phenomena continued until Parsons was forced to move with his daughter into a house in Covent Garden. Even there the raps continued.

The much maligned Kent went to Law. This forced Parsons into the position of proving the ghost was genuine. Told that her parents would be gaoled if no raps were heard that night, Elizabeth unsuccessfully tried to fake them. Next day, the newspapers were informing their readers that the famous Cock Lane ghost was a fraud.

After the actual hearing, Parsons was sentenced to two years imprisonment. The hapless Revd Moore and a colleague involved were ordered to pay almost £600 in damages to Kent — a massive sum at the time. Oliver Goldsmith, the poet, produced a satirical pamphlet on the whole affair and a play called *The Drummer or The Haunted House* drew huge crowds to the Covent Garden Playhouse.

A little over half a century later, public attention had switched to America where the case of the 'Bell Witch' was in full swing.

It began quietly enough in the home of Tennessee farmer John Bell. First sounds of scratchings from inside the walls, were dismissed, reasonably enough, as rats. Then came the noise of a dog scratching on the floor, a bird flapping against the ceiling, two dogs fighting . . .

Although no one could see these animals, the conviction was that they must actually *be* animals and no one paid a great deal of attention. Occasionally, members of the Bell family would get up in the night to investigate and the sounds would immediately cease. This is animal behaviour and tended to confirm the early suspicions. Unfortunately it is also poltergeist behaviour. Soon bedclothes were being pulled off, less animal-like noises being heard, stones being thrown and furniture toppled.

It was a particularly serious manifestation and one which lasted well beyond the few months typical to poltergeist cases. For a year the house resounded to the noises, which sometimes became so violent that the walls shook. Two of the nine Bell children, Betsy, and Richard Williams, complained that an invisible hand had pulled their hair in the night. Betsy seemed to be a particular prey to persecution by the entity, which took to slapping her face and scratching her body, even when she was away from home.

Things went from bad to worse. Weird lights flitted about the yard after dark. Stones and pieces of wood were thrown at the children. Visitors were punched and slapped. The entity found its voice and made comments in a low whisper. John Bell developed a curious affliction of his tongue and jaw which forced him to miss meals for days at a time.

The voice phenomena increased in volume, then in number. The original voice which first identified itself as an Indian, then as a witch called Kate Batts, was joined by others calling themselves Jerusalem, Mathematics, Cypocryphy and Blackdog.

With them came a distinct smell of whisky.

This collection of witches detested John Bell, but seemed quite fond of other members of his household: they materialized a basket of fruit for Betsy's birthday and pulled the children's sled around the house in winter.

John Bell, by contrast, was persecuted to his grave. For three years he was forced to endure constant torments. His shoes were jerked from his feet, his face and head punched, his body sent into convulsions. He was pursued by ghostly laughter, derisive comments and songs. A week before Christmas, 1820, the family found him in a coma. The 'witch' claimed to have poisoned him in his sleep, using the contents of a bottle in the medicine cupboard. The bottle did prove to contain poison: in an experiment, the local doctor used it to kill a cat. Bell himself died the next day.

The Bell witch remained, although the manifestations were now much less violent. Overall the haunting lasted four years. In 1821, a burst of smoke and explosion from the chimney heralded the witch's departure. There was a minor manifestation of poltergeist activity in the house seven years later, but it did not develop into anything spectacular.

America was also the scene of the most influential poltergeist occurrence in history. It occurred at Hydesville, New York in the farmhouse of the Fox family. During March of 1848 raps were heard in the night and the two young Fox sisters, Margaret and Kate discovered that if they snapped their fingers, the ghostly raps would imitate them. A neighbour suggested establishing communication using a code based on 'one rap for yes; two raps for no'. As we have seen, this sort of thing had been tried successfully before, but now it was an idea whose time had come. As more and more information was obtained from the entity (which followed the Fox sisters around rather than remaining confined to the house) the girls became the first mediums of a craze which swept through America, then crossed the Atlantic to become the fascination of Britain and Europe. The craze was, of course, Spiritualism, a minority religion which flourishes to this day.

But if the Fox case was the most influential poltergeist happening, the most important in our present study is one we have not yet examined. The first account of it was published as long ago as 1666 by the Revd Joseph Glanvill, who had personal experience of the phenomenon.

The case was that of the 'Drummer of Tidworth'. It is sufficiently well documented and interesting to warrant a brief chapter of its own.

3
The Phantom Drummer

A scholarly cleric, the Revd Joseph Glanvill, published the first account of the Phantom Drummer of Tidworth in 1666. He had a personal interest. Glanvill described how he went to the house which then stood on the site of the present Zouche Manor in Wiltshire. There he found 'two modest little girls in bed between seven and eleven years old'. He also heard a mysterious scratching sound from behind the bolster.

Glanvill was satisfied the noise was not made by the girls, since their hands were in full view. Nor could he find any cause elsewhere in the room. What he did find, a little later, was a linen bag with, apparently, something like a rat or a mouse moving about inside it. Glanvill drew the bag inside out, but it was empty.

The account, which is noteworthy for its reasonable tone and attention to detail, does not mark the end of this peculiar case; nor even the beginning. It actually started on a March day in 1661 when John Mompesson, a magistrate, visited the village of Ludgershall in east Wiltshire.

Mompesson seems to have been a man short on temper and long on self-importance. He became so irritated by the sound of drumming he heard in the street that he brought the matter up with the local constable. The constable informed him that the cause was a tinker named William Drury, who had arrived in the village a few days earlier. Drury, added the constable, had requested public assistance on the strength of various papers signed by eminent magistrates. The request had been refused: the constable suspected the papers were forgeries.

Mompesson promptly ordered that Drury be arraigned before him and discovered that the constable's suspicions were well justified – the papers were forged. Mompesson committed Drury to remain in custody until the next sitting of the Bench and confiscated his drum. The loss of the drum seems to have upset Drury far more than the prospect of the gaol term. But he pleaded for the return of the instrument without success. The case was temporarily closed and Mompesson went on his way.

The constable may have been a more charitable soul than the magistrate for he seems to have been deliberately careless in keeping an eye on Drury. In any event the tinker escaped – without, however, managing to salvage his precious drum. For want of anything better to do with it, the Court Bailiff dispatched the drum to Mompesson. It arrived at his home in Tidworth while he was away in London.

The magistrate returned to a mystery. Servants assured him the house had been assailed by violent raps and knocks for three nights running. Mompesson seems to have suspected villainy at work (magistrates then were no more popular in certain quarters than they are today). He went to bed that night with a loaded pistol for comfort.

Sure enough, the noises started. Mompesson leaped up brandishing his pistol, and ran into the next room where the sounds were coming from. To his annoyance, the noises moved to another room. Mompesson followed. The noises moved again. And again. And again. Eventually when the sounds seemed to move outside, Mompesson gave up and went back to bed. The sound continued. Now, amongst them, the magistrate could distinguish drumbeats.

The noises returned the next night and the next. Often they went on for hours on end, still without anyone being able to discover their source. They stopped for a period of three weeks (perhaps coincidentally, Mrs Mompesson was in labour during this time) but resumed again louder than ever.

As a poltergeist case, this one followed a familiar pattern, growing steadily worse long before it got better. The noises, which now comprised frequent and recognizable drumming, took to following the Mompesson children around. Small articles began to move around of their own accord: a manservant spent some time in a tug of war with the entity for possession of a breadboard. When a minister arrived to pray for the safety of the children, the noises grew louder than ever and were accompanied by a suitably demonic smell of burning sulphur.

This sort of nonsense and a great deal more went on for two full years. The Mompesson house became a supernatural fairground of raps, knocks, bangs, slamming doors and mysterious lights. One morning Mompesson found his horse on its back with its hind hoof jammed into its mouth. A visitor had coins in his pocket turned black. Another had his sword snatched away. The entity attacked a local blacksmith with a pair of pincers.

The thing, like others before it, became vocal. Glanvill claimed it shouted 'A witch! A witch!' at least a hundred times. Its brutality towards animals seems to have been sensed by the animals themselves, for Glanvill found his horse sweating in terror. (The beast actually died soon afterwards.) Mompesson, meanwhile, was treated to the spectacle of a glaring phantom beside his bed — which faded away without offering him more harm than the original fright. His children were not so lucky. They had the contents of ashcans and chamberpots emptied into their beds.

How the manifestation ended is not particularly clear. Perhaps it simply faded away like many another poltergeist. Certainly by the time Glanvill published his account, peace had been restored.

So far, of course, the case differs very little from various other poltergeist manifestations we have already studied. But there is a postscript to the whole affair that makes it singularly interesting.

In 1663, two years after the trouble started, the vagrant William Drury stole a pig at Gloucester and was arrested and gaoled for his enterprise. While he languished in prison, a friend came to visit him and Drury enquired about the news from Wiltshire.

At first the friend did not know what he was talking about. Then Drury asked if he had not heard about the disturbances in the house at Tidworth. Since by now the disturbances were common knowledge, the friend admitted that he had. At which point Drury admitted he had been their cause. He had, he said, 'plagued' Mompesson and would continue to do so until the magistrate made restitution for taking away his drum.

It was an incautious claim, for whether it was true or not (a point we shall soon be examining) it led to his trial for witchcraft at Salisbury. In an earlier age — or even in his own — he might have been hanged or burned. In fact, though found guilty, he was merely deported. Glanvill claims the haunting of Tidworth stopped as soon as Drury was out of the country.

Drury's admission is an interesting development: the first time, so far as I am aware, that anyone claimed to have deliberately and consciously *created* a poltergeist. The statement may, of course, have been bravado, the empty bluster of a man so far down that he would seize on any coincidence in order to re-establish his self-esteem.

But what if it were not coincidence? What if Drury had a talent for creating poltergeists and sending them to do his bidding?

4
Elemental Servants

The question ending the last chapter was not rhetorical. Some ten years ago, I found myself caught up in a situation with important implications. It suggests there are certain individuals with an ability to despatch an invisible entity to do their bidding. And in this case at least, this entity behaved as poltergeists have always behaved.

In the account of the situation which follows, I have changed names and locations to make the participants unrecognizable. But these are the only changes. Nothing has been falsified, nothing added for the sake of dramatic effect.

The situation arose when a professional writer approached me to arrange for her to interview a witch. (I had been doing some radio broadcasts on the subject.) Although my contacts in the Craft were few, there was one man I felt might make an interesting story. For the sake of this account, I will call him George Danford.

Danford was an oddity in the occult field in that he had a scientific/technical background and training. At an early stage in his career, he had 'dropped out' to pursue esoteric studies, specializing mainly in poltergeist phenomena and witchcraft. In relation to the latter interest, he was a loner: he joined no covens, nor thought of himself as belonging to any of the various 'traditions' which go to make up the Craft in Britain today. I had known him for many years and was always impressed by the breadth of his research into these curious subjects, and by his refreshing habit of applying scientific criteria to them.

I approached Danford and found he was perfectly willing to

be interviewed. When I conveyed this news to my writer friend (let us call her Sheila Thoms) she was at once pleased and a little nervous. She had never interviewed a witch before and wondered if I would come along to keep her company. Although I assured her she was in no occult danger from Danford, I agreed to be present.

It took place in the study of Danford's home and lasted a full afternoon. Sheila and Danford hit it off well from the very beginning, so that I was quickly relegated to the background while they talked intensely about Danford's career and interests.

When the interview proper was over, Danford produced tea and the conversation continued. By this stage it had turned to esoteric healing methods and Sheila Thoms was discussing a personal problem which had been troubling her greatly for several months. The problem was an unsightly skin complaint. It had begun abruptly and so far resisted all attempts by the medical profession to find a cure. Did Danford, she wondered, know of anything that might work? Some witchcraft technique, for instance? Danford explained that he was not a healer, but promised to look into the matter and do what he could. There the matter was left.

The meeting between Sheila Thoms and Danford took place on a Friday. The following Monday I called at Sheila Thoms' home to be greeted by her in a state of high excitement. The skin condition was improving! I looked closely and found she was right. The disease was certainly not yet cured, but there was a very definite improvement. I asked if I might call again to monitor progress, since the development intrigued me.

By the Thursday following the interview, Sheila Thoms' skin was clear for the first time in months. She was convinced the cure was Danford's doing, but wanted to wait a little while before contacting him in case it proved to be one of those spontaneous, but sadly temporary, remissions which sometimes occur with such complaints. I agreed that this seemed a prudent course. The sudden cure could have been coincidental. Danford had, after all, laid no claim to healing talents: merely promised to look into the matter and do his best.

But over the course of that day, events convinced me Danford was indeed involved; and in a very peculiar manner.

Ms Thoms and I had an appointment that evening and she suggested I come in and wait while she got ready. She went upstairs to change. I was in the kitchen of her home when I heard a sudden loud crash outside the door. I ran into the hallway and found Sheila Thoms lying at the bottom of the stairs. She was unhurt but very shocked. She had been on the way down when someone had pushed her so violently that she had fallen. I helped her into the kitchen, then went upstairs to find the intruder. There was no one there. We were alone in the house. Nor was there any indication of any break-in.

I returned to the kitchen to question her about her experience. She was quite adamant that she had been pushed: she had felt the hands distinctly. My suggestions that she might have fainted were angrily dismissed. I could only assure her that whoever had pushed her was no longer in the house. Eventually she calmed down enough to go back upstairs to take a bath.

I heard another scream from upstairs. Sheila Thoms appeared almost at once, wearing a dressing gown. She was close to hysterics. While in the bath, something she could not see had burned her arm, then bitten her on the leg. After the bite, she had clapped her hand to her leg and felt a small, furry (but quite invisible) animal on her thigh.

I examined her arm and her leg. The outer forearm showed a small, but perfectly distinct circular burn mark, as if someone had stubbed out a lighted cigarette there. There were four red puncture marks on the inner thigh, similar to the bite of a rat or other small animal.

Although I said nothing to Sheila Thoms at the time, I had my own suspicions about the cause of all this. The following day I called on Danford.

One of the first things he asked me about was the progress of my friend's skin complaint. I told him it seemed to be cured and asked if we had him to thank for it. He said he had tried a small experiment in the hope of achieving a cure. I asked him what technique he had used. Danford said he had tried to send a poltergeist.

Unlikely though this claim might sound, there can be no doubt that: (a) Sheila Thoms experienced phenomena identical to those typically reported in poltergeist hauntings; (b) The problem stopped completely once Danford was alerted; (c) Ms Thoms' skin complaint ceased to trouble her during the time of the pseudo-poltergeist haunting; and (d) The skin complaint returned shortly after Danford agreed to 'call off' his mischievous healing entity.

I mention this case because of my firsthand knowledge, not because it is necessarily unique. There is a widespread folk tradition of secret techniques used to 'call up' and command invisible entities. The tradition has not, of course, been taken seriously by historians since the techniques are supposedly 'magical' or 'occult'. Yet many 'magical' techniques *do* work, as anyone who has taken the trouble to investigate them will confirm. Some — like hypnosis — have even managed to achieve widespread recognition.

The problem with the tradition is that the 'entities' involved are not called poltergeists. They are referred to as 'elementals' or sometimes 'familiars'. Nonetheless, elementals and familiars have often been described as behaving in ways very similar to the classical poltergeist.

Nowhere is the tradition stronger than in the history of witchcraft. A legal treatise, written by William West of the Inner Temple in 1594 actually defines a witch as follows:

> . . . she which being [d]eluded by a league [covenant] made with the devil through his perswasion, inspiration and [juggling], thinketh she can designe what maner of evil things soever, either by thought or imprication, as to shake the air with lightnings and thunder, to cause hail and tempests, to remove grene come or trees to another place, *to be* [carried by] *her familiar* which hath taken upon him the deceiptful shape of a goate, swine or calfe, etc. into some mountaine farre distant, in a wonderfull short space of time.

There are, of course, serious difficulties in accepting much of

the Court evidence with regard to witchcraft. Even in England,
where there is no indication of actual torture of suspected witches,
the accused were often ill-treated. The Revd John Gaule, in 1646
wrote an interesting account of the activities of the notorious
'Witchfinder General', Matthew Hopkins, which described how
one suspect was examined:

> Having taken the suspected witch, she is placed in the middle
> of a room upon a stool or table, cross-legged, or in some other
> uneasy posture, to which, if she submits not, she is then bound
> with cords; there she is watched and kept without meat or
> sleep for the space of twenty-four hours.

Those deprived of sleep and food, imprisoned and constantly
watched, have a tendency to admit to charges they might
otherwise deny; and the 'binding with cords in uncomfortable
positions' was by no means the worst of the ill treatment, even
though it fell short of what was legally admitted as torture.

Nonetheless, a careful examination of the records produces
some surprises. In 1612, for example, a woman named Elizabeth
Haynes confessed spontaneously to 'entertaining imps in the
likeness of kitlings'. In this instance, ill treatment is highly unlikely
since there is no indication at all of any legal conspiracy to convict.
(The Grand Jury actually chose to reject her confession and threw
out the case.)

If this were an isolated instance, we might imagine Goodwife
Haynes to be deluded or insane. But it was not. At the same
Assizes in Lancashire, a second accused, Bridget Weaver, confessed
that she had 'cherished an imp'. Like Haynes, Weaver was
disbelieved and acquitted. At Norfolk Summer Assizes in 1645,
Anna Palmer was also acquitted, despite freely confessing to
'having imps like turkey cocks'.

Free confessions like these — and the three given represent only
the very small tip of a very large iceberg — suggest that a number
of individuals believed themselves capable of controlling 'imps'
or 'familiars'. We may, like the jurors of Lancashire and Norfolk,
choose to dismiss individual claims, but it is very difficult to

ignore the *totality* of such evidence. Even when the liars and the lunatics are weeded out, there are still more than enough left to give us the uneasy suspicion that something very odd was going on.

In the circumstances, it is worth looking a little more closely at the 'imps', 'familiars' and 'elementals' of witchcraft. Once again, unfortunately, the examination is beset with difficulties. Some of these have already manifested themselves.

Anna Palmer claimed her 'imps' were 'like turkey cocks'. John Gaule's account of the Hopkins examination goes on to say:

> . . . within that time (the twenty-four hours) they shall see her imp come and suck. A little hole is likewise made in the door for the imp to come in at; and lest it might come in some less discernible shape, they that watch are taught to be ever and anon sweeping the room, and if they see any spiders or flies, to kill them. And if they cannot kill them, then they may be sure they are her imps.

However open-minded we may strive to be, it is clearly impossible to take this sort of thing seriously. The tradition that the witch's imp or familiar took physical form in the shape of an animal, bird or insect, obtaining sustenance from the witch's own body, is now almost universally dismissed. The problem is that the imps themselves have been dismissed along with it. This may be taking things a bit too far.

If we look towards the evidence of what witches were supposed to do with their imps, a slightly more credible picture emerges.

At Witham Summer Sessions in 1584, for example, a yeoman named Edmund Mansell was accused of despatching an imp to set fire to a barn and stables, destroying property to the value of £49 10s in the process. Seventeenth-century depositions preserved in the British Museum include that of a John Waller who, while watching a suspect witch, saw a door 'creep' open of its own accord. Another, dealing with the case of Anna Marsh of Tattingstone, states that the clothes of a witness's child were set on fire by invisible means.

Firesetting and objects which 'creep' or move of their own accord are, of course, typical poltergeist hauntings. The deposition of Maria Brame, which describes how 'imps' came and 'scared her out of her sleep' sounds suspiciously like poltergeists as well. And the accusation of John Easte against Susanna Stegold that she sent three imps to torment her husband to death sounds less ridiculous when we remember the fate of John Bell, similarly tormented to death by a poltergeist centuries later.

Perhaps the most intriguing account of all is the confession of Margaret Bayts, who was at work when she felt 'a thinge' nip her on the leg — an experience which was repeated some time later while she was visiting a churchyard. There is no indication in the early part of her deposition that she actually saw this entity, although she certainly felt it. Later she described it as 'like a mouse', although here again it is far from clear whether she was speaking of its appearance or its feel.

This deposition, written three centuries ago, almost exactly mirrors the experience of Sheila Thoms when she was, apparently, visited by the entity sent to cure her skin problem. Where the cases differ is that Margaret Bayts claimed to have befriended the mischievous creature by feeding it and consequently became a witch in the process.

That imps or familiars could be 'sent' or even handed on as gifts from one person to another, was a firm belief in times past. The Court depositions are full of incidental details like the claim of Joane Balls to have sent two imps to her daughter, with the admonition not to be afraid of them.

Even outside the troubled annals of witchcraft there are clear indications of a lasting belief in controllable entities which have themselves the smell of poltergeists.

As long ago as 1458, a Jewish Qabalist penned a very curious manuscript in Hebrew as a magical textbook for his younger son. An eighteenth-century French copy of this manuscript was discovered in the *Bibliotheque de l'Arsenal* during the Victorian era. It was subsequently translated into English by S. L. MacGregor Mathers, under the title *The Book of the Sacred Magic of Abra-Melin the Mage*.

When I first heard of this work some twenty years ago, copies were virtually unobtainable. Since then, however, a facsimile edition has been brought out by an American publisher, while in 1976, the Aquarian Press made it available in paperback format.

The book itself is odd, even in a category noted for oddities. After an interesting historical preamble in which Abra-Melin explains that tradition precludes him from teaching his second son the Qabalah, the author outlines a single, lengthy magical operation designed as a working substitute. This operation, which takes several months to perform, promises to place the student in contact with his 'Holy Guardian Angel.'

Unlike many of the ancient grimoires (which are largely collections of repulsive superstitions) this one seems to get results, possibly because the techniques involved are actually an unorthodox form of yoga. At least one author has published his own account of experiences produced by the operation; and I have personal reason to believe that the book contains information of practical as well as historical interest.

My own involvement with the Abra-Melin system arose when I was contacted by a man I shall call Benson, who had been experimenting with it and needed an outside evaluation of his results.

It may be as well to explain that the book itself is divided into two parts. The first gives details of the Guardian Angel operation. The second describes a series of 'magic squares'. Abra-Melin warns that no one should attempt to use the squares without first undertaking the Angelic operation. Benson ignored this warning. He had begun the full operation, but abandoned it after a few weeks — well short of completion — and turned instead to use of the squares.

Whatever one thinks about the warning, he seemed to be getting results. The relevant squares had been followed by financial windfalls, success in Court actions, even an unexpected love affair. His problem was that he could not quite decide whether the 'results' were actual or coincidental.

Anyone with a rational frame of mind would find it easy to

sympathize with his plight. The whole thrust of twentieth-century culture suggests that magic is nonsense and those who practise it are either stupid, superstitious or deluded. Benson felt himself to be none of these things, but was nonetheless worried that he might be well on the way to self-deception.

After writing several books on the subject, I can hardly claim to have an open mind about magic. My experience clearly suggests (to my own satisfaction at least) that there are occult techniques which produce observable results, even though the actual *mechanism* is not always recognized or understood.

This does not lead me to accept every miraculous claim made by occult practitioners. My experience, regrettably, has also been that there are few fields of human endeavour so riddled with muddled thinking. Nevertheless, I do accept that there are individuals able to extend their perceptions further than the average. These individuals are known as 'psychics' and I am delighted to know one or two whom I accept utterly as genuine. I took one of these psychics to meet Benson and observe while he wrote a magical Abra-Melin square.

At the risk of making this account more complex than it deserves, I had best mention that my psychical companion had her own preconceptions concerning 'magical squares'. As an author herself, she had been engaged in research which showed such squares, converted to their geometrical equivalents, had been used in pre-Christian temple design. Because of this, she was not overly impressed by the notion that they might have any 'magical' usage.

Nonetheless, she observed psychically while Benson produced a series of squares in accordance with the Abra-Melin instructions. In each case, to her own surprise, she found that entities became immediately manifest to her second sight. Although neither of us had, at the time, any knowledge of which squares Benson was producing, he went into more detail later, confirming that the entities 'seen' were similar to those traditionally associated with the squares.

Despite the nature of this experiment, I was quite prepared to accept it as substantiating the reality of Benson's results. As a sidelight, it also provided firsthand substantiation of Danford's claim that even today it remains possible to make use of invisible entities — exactly as occult tradition has always claimed.

But the controlled use of invisible entities seems to be rare. The same cannot be said for the spontaneous occurrence of poltergeist phenomena in the present age, as the next chapter will demonstrate.

5

The Poltergeists Among Us

Some quirk of human psychology makes it easier to believe that ghosts existed centuries ago than that they exist today. But when the ghosts concerned are poltergeists, there is abundant evidence that they are as active now as they ever were in any bygone age.

In February 1974, the Oxford Institute of Psychophysical Research issued an appeal for personal accounts of ghostly experiences. By the beginning of April, they had 1,500 statements to sort out, with more coming in each day. Even at that point, the response was three times greater than they had anticipated. Replies were coming in from all over the world — Korea, West Africa, India, Australia, New Zealand, as well as Britain. Not all the accounts were of poltergeists, but many were.

The sheer volume of modern poltergeist cases is ably illustrated by what happened when the *News of the World* ran an investigation into the subject in June 1978. Within a week of the published report, the newspaper's offices were flooded with readers' own accounts. Several of these were followed up and published. They make interesting reading.

Among them was the story of an Oxfordshire builder, Ken Preedy, who specialized in the renovation of old cottages. It does not sound like a particularly dangerous occupation, but Mr Preedy's experiences suggest that old cottages are sometimes the focus of poltergeist activity. In one cottage, his tools kept disappearing or being moved mysteriously to different rooms. At another, the poltergeist activity was more open — a shovel was thrown at him by invisible hands!

From Leicester came a report of an old house (now demolished) in which phantom footsteps were heard and pictures flung from the walls. There was also a pervasive smell of gas, although investigation showed no indication of the source. (Bad smells are quite common in poltergeist cases. In one I investigated personally, the stench was so strong that the family hired workmen to investigate the drains. The plumbing proved to be in order but when ornaments began to be thrown about the house, it was realized that the smell was only the beginning of a poltergeist manifestation.)

Not all – indeed not most – of the reported cases were associated with old houses. A Cheshire woman, Mrs E. Butterfield, wrote to describe what happened when her teenage daughter took a bath.

After the girl had finished, Mrs Butterfield went into the bathroom and was annoyed to find the bath still filled, and that wet towels were scattered across the floor. Parents of teenage children will readily appreciate that poltergeists were not the first explanation that sprang into her mind. But her daughter denied leaving the bathroom in the state Mrs Butterfield had found it in. The room was tidied and the bath drained with both mother and daughter present. When Mrs Butterfield's husband came home, he found it in its original state, with the bath again filled.

The mystery was solved – or possibly deepened – when noises began and clothes were mysteriously pulled out of drawers. The Butterfields had a poltergeist. They eventually moved house.

Like unpleasant smells, the abrupt beginning of a poltergeist case is not unusual. If anything, it is the norm. Sometimes, however, the initial manifestation does not develop any further; like the case of Londoner Mrs J. Redshaw, who was putting fruit into a bowl when it jumped out again and rolled away. Nothing more happened, but the single incident was a classical example of poltergeist activity.

If the entities can appear at any time, they can also appear at any place, and in any country. This was brought home to a family named LaRue when they moved into a seventeen-room hilltop mansion in Frankfort, Michigan, USA. The house had a reputation of being haunted (the previous occupants called the ghost 'Mary') and all reports point towards the haunting being classified as poltergeist.

In the LaRue mansion, lights began to switch on and off without human aid. Doors opened and closed of their own accord. Footsteps sounded in empty rooms. A heavy dining table was shifted from its place to end up blocking the bay windows. A typewriter began to tap all by itself. Dishes banged and clattered in the small hours of the morning while everyone was in bed. Perhaps most impressive of all was the heavy picture which climbed up the wall for two feet before falling on the floor: two people watched it do so.

With commendable scepticism, Mrs Kaye LaRue states she 'neither believes nor disbelieves in spirits'. Not everyone can afford the luxury of disbelief. A Mrs Docking of Streatham, London, felt obliged to write to a newspaper to describe her own poltergeist happening. According to the published account, she was sitting quietly at home when all the doors opened abruptly – including cupboard and oven doors. She closed them up again and even moved the furniture around, but the doors continued to open of their own accord for several weeks.

When the poltergeist abruptly changed tactics (by pushing Mrs Docking out of bed onto the floor) she lost patience and ordered it to leave. Curiously, she had no further trouble.

Some poltergeists are actually at home in crowds. In January, 1980, the *News of the World* reported the case of Jim Fay's busy pub, The Crown, where furniture was switched around, ornaments knocked off walls, kettles turned on and off and money thrown about.

Press people are considerably more cynical about such reports than one might imagine from reading the papers. Nonetheless in this instance, a *News of the World* photographer, David Hooley, went on record with a statement that he had actually witnessed poltergeist phenomena in The Crown. A leather whip hanging on the wall began to quiver, then its lash swung round as the temperature of the room abruptly plummeted. Hooley was, he later said, 'glad to get out'.

In circumstances like this, it is not unusual for those plagued by poltergeists to conclude they are a prey to an evil spirit. This was certainly the case for a young Irish couple named in published accounts only as 'Betty and John'. They found their new home in the extensive Ballymun housing estate, North Dublin, to be 'cold as an ice box' even with the central heating running. There was also, they noticed, a bad smell.

Problems of this sort were not new to them. The 'evil spirit' had been following them about for some time. It first manifested when they were living in a flat in Blackpool, England, with tapping noises, the sound of footsteps and banging at their door. At that time, they concluded that the flat was haunted and left. They returned to their native Ireland and took up residence in a house on Dublin's North Circular Road. Within a week, the poltergeist moved in as well. This time it did more than knock. Plaster exploded off the walls, pictures were turned the wrong way round and the bed was lifted off the floor.

They moved again to Ballymun and achieved a degree of peace for four years. Then the problem started up again.

Another Irish case demonstrating that poltergeists are still among us was that concerning the rural home of Mr James McGrath in County Westmeath. The case was investigated by representatives of various media, including Irish Television, but perhaps the most comprehensive report appeared in the local paper, the *Westmeath Examiner*, two of whose reporters experienced the phenomena for themselves.

The trouble started in August 1981 when the McGrath family noticed noises coming from the roof. These were not particularly loud nor disturbing and were put down to natural causes. Over the next few months, however, the phenomena began to manifest more strongly, with lights being switched on and off and various small items moved out of their normal places.

The manifestations died down before Christmas, but began again in the New Year. Personal items began to be moved to different rooms, while there were violent noises in the outside yard, where buckets and milk churn lids were tossed around. The most consistent incident was the throwing of stones onto the roof.

As Roman Catholics, the McGraths decided to call on help from their church and the house was subsequently blessed by a priest. This did nothing to stop the manifestations, which continued ten days later with a loud thump on the roof.

John McGrath, a brother of the owner, watched on a still night while an outside cable moved violently as if someone were swinging on it. A plastic bucket, left beside an outbuilding, moved towards him of its own accord, stopping less than three yards from his feet. McGrath's daughter Ann was bringing water into the house when a kitchen brush (kept inside the house) fell off the roof and struck her on the head.

Shoes proved a common plaything for the poltergeist. They were frequently moved about inside the house and on at least one occasion a pair was transported outside to be left near their owner's car. James McGrath personally witnessed churn lids spinning in the yard.

The poltergeist (as happens often in such cases) proved dangerously amenable to suggestion. A casual remark by one of the family that it was amazing how no windows had been broken was instantly followed by the breaking of a bedroom window.

Other phenomena included the opening of doors and the movement of heavy logs.

Perhaps the most peculiar of all poltergeist cases reported in recent years is that sited at the home of Kent housewife, Pamela Masters. Here the manifestations began in 1976, since when, according to Mrs Masters, 'none of us has had a decent night's sleep for fear that something else will happen.' Like the McGraths in Ireland, the Masters family would wake up in the morning to find objects moved out of place all over the house. On one occasion a coffee cup was wrenched from the hands of the person drinking from it. Mysterious drawings appeared overnight on walls.

All these are typical enough poltergeist phenomena. What makes the Kent case unusual was the unwitting involvement of two internationally famous American television actors.

Mrs Masters' 19-year-old daughter Karen was a fan of Paul

Michael Glaser and David Soul, actors perhaps best known for their portrayal of the police detectives Starsky and Hutch in the television series of the same name. There were dozens of pictures of them in the house – so many in fact that Mrs Masters complained to her daughter about them.

'The next thing I knew I saw Paul Michael Glaser standing there,' Mrs Masters told a reporter later. 'I thought I was daydreaming. But from that day onwards I kept seeing Glaser or David Soul around the house.'

The ghostly visitation of the TV stars would stretch credibility to its limits were it not for the fact that Mrs Masters was not the only one to see them. At least five other witnesses had the same experience, making this one of the most peculiar contemporary poltergeist cases on record.

6
Ghosts . . . or Mindpower?

Anyone reading this far must be wondering how seriously to take the foregoing reports. The contemporary accounts have been drawn in the main from newspaper reports – not always the most reliable of sources – while historical cases are, by definition, beyond scientific investigation.

These are very reasonable objections. But the point is not the validity of any particular case. The point is that for centuries past and in the present day, poltergeist phenomena have been a fact of human life. Not all reported poltergeist cases are genuine, of course, any more than all reported motor accidents are genuine. But most are. If the sheer volume of testimony did not bear this out, then the patient work of psychical investigators working under the most rigorous scientific disciplines must confirm it absolutely.

Cases similar to those outlined have been attracting serious investigative attention for a little more than a century now. Some of the phenomena was found to be due to perfectly natural causes – airlocked plumbing, for example, can cause quite fearsome metallic banging noises, while shifting foundations have set many an ornament toppling. Fraud has been detected in certain instances – the unscrupulous have always been willing to create a few ghostly diversions for the sake of personal notoriety or gain.

But when fraud and mistaken identity are both ruled out, the poltergeist survives. A *single* 'haunted house' in North London drew these comments from experts of impeccable credentials:

Surgeon Ian Fletcher: 'Happenings in that house are very strongly suggestive of paranormal phenomena . . . I feel there is a poltergeist presence in the house.'

Engineer David Anette: 'There is definitely something odd which I cannot explain.'

Physics Assistant David Robertson: 'Once I saw a sideboard lift up at an angle and fall face down on the floor. Many strange things are unexplained.'

Author Guy Lyon Playfair: 'I personally have witnessed five incidents for which no reasonable normal explanation has yet been suggested. Each was recorded on tape.

Investigator Maurice Grosse, called in by the Society for Psychical Research, went on record with a written statement that he had personally witnessed:

1. a slipper thrown across a bedroom;
2. a box of cushions thrown at him;
3. a lampshade tilting to an angle of 45 degrees, then straightening up again;
4. a settee thrown in the air and overturned;
5. a door opening and closing of its own accord;
6. marbles and plastic blocks materializing from walls and windows before flying across a room;
7. a teapot 'dancing' on a kitchen cabinet.

In face of the overwhelming evidence from experts and lay people alike, the question is no longer whether people are telling the truth about poltergeists, but rather what causes the phenomena in the first place.

This question has absorbed a good many scientific minds. While the lay person may be perfectly satisfied to talk of ghosts, scientists, by and large, are not. Once early investigators satisfied themselves that *something* was going on, they bent their attention towards finding the cause — without preconceptions.

By the turn of the present century, certain common denominators began to be noticeable in a majority of the poltergeist cases studied. The first was the fact that the noisy 'ghosts' seemed to haunt people rather than places.

This may sound unimportant, but even in itself it tends to set poltergeists apart from other ghostly phenomena, which are almost always linked to specific sites.

There have been, of course, several poltergeist cases associated with places — the notorious and well-documented Borley Rectory is a classic example — but in the main, a poltergeist seems to attach itself to a particular family or individual. Moving house (as we have already seen) will not necessarily — not even usually — get rid of the ghost. The young Irish couple mentioned in the previous chapter actually moved country. Their invisible tormentor followed them like a faithful pet.

Another common denominator to emerge was the way those plagued by poltergeists seemed able to avoid serious injury. The Bell witch, which eventually poisoned poor John Bell, is a rare exception to the rule. In almost every other instance, injuries sustained during a poltergeist haunting tend to be very minor indeed.

This too is more peculiar than it sounds. Poltergeist manifestations are often characterized by extreme violence. Knocks and raps can reach such force that walls shake. Heavy furniture can be flung around energetically. When communication is established with a poltergeist, the entity will frequently claim impressively evil credentials — as the spirit of a murderer, for instance, or even a demon. But in the vast majority of cases, the most evil action these 'demons' can conceive is to keep decent people awake at night.

There is no argument about the fact that poltergeists have enough energy to cause very considerable injury indeed. When an entity can levitate a heavy settee, it takes little extra effort to let it drop on someone's head. Yet in the majority of cases, this sort of thing does not happen. What *does* happen much more often is the *appearance* of violence. Stones or heavy ornaments will be thrown at poltergeist victims; but these miraculously miss their targets by a hairsbreadth. And in the few instances where the missile has hit home, it has done so with minimum damage — often without any damage at all. The author

Colin Wilson, interviewing the victims of poltergeist attack, was told that while the missile *appeared* to be thrown with great violence, it actually struck them with almost no force at all. It was as if the object had not actually been thrown but *carried.*

This curiousity shows itself even in the unfortunate Bell case. Here the victim died eventually and the 'ghost' took credit for his death. But was the claim to have poisoned Bell another example of poltergeist tall tales? The invisible entities which plagued the Bell household had ample opportunity — and apparently ample ability — to kill off their victim long before he actually expired. The 'witch' showed it could wield an axe: why not, then, use it on John Bell's skull? Or if this proved too difficult, why not simply push him downstairs?

Yet while Bell was persecuted to distraction, no attack of this sort occurred. The poltergeists contented themselves with childish pranks and threats. Perhaps after years of this persecution, John Bell simply decided he had had enough and took his own life. If there was poison in the medicine cabinet, he may have concluded it was better to end it all than endure more years of torment. Once the man was obviously dying, the entity may have laid claim to murder as such entities have always laid claim to grandiose acts of evil without the slightest real evidence to support their word.

Careful study of poltergeist hauntings leads one to the conclusion that such cases are not always what they seem. The Bell poltergeist claimed to be a witch. The poltergeist which knocked on the door of the Fox sisters claimed to be the spirit of a pedlar. Other poltergeists have claimed to be Satan and a whole collection of lesser devils. In recent years there have even been poltergeist manifestations claiming to be aliens from outer space. The central *phenomenon* remains the same. It is the poltergeists' own explanations which vary.

The third — and possibly most important — common denominator was found to be the commonplace connection with one or more young people: usually adolescent, usually female.

Although our case histories were chosen at random, this aspect shows through clearly in many of them. The Bell family comprised nine children, including Betsy, who was just entering puberty when the manifestations began. Despite his theories about witchcraft, Samuel Wesley could not help but notice his poltergeist problems seemed to be in some way associated with his 19-year-old daughter Hetty, who often trembled in her sleep before the noises began. The Revd Glanvill, who came to investigate the famous 'Drummer' found 'modest little girls' in the bed. The Fox sisters were in their teens when their phantom pedlar first came calling. And so on.

This is not, of course, to suggest that all poltergeists are somehow associated with teenage girls. Some manifestly are not. But like the stranger at the feast, young girls (and less often young boys) were so frequently a part of the background to poltergeist hauntings that the experts began to wonder if there might be a direct link between the two.

Any theory of any sort is only as strong as its exceptions; and there are a wealth of exceptions to the rule that where you find a poltergeist there too you will find an adolescent. Nonetheless, the commonplace link set the investigators thinking. Before long a theory emerged. Broadly stated, the theory was this: whatever they seem to be, poltergeists are not ghosts, not spirits of the dead, not alien entities from mythology like demons or devils; rather, poltergeists are unusual creations of the human mind.

We need to be careful about that last part. No one is saying that poltergeists are imaginary, or even hallucinatory. The phenomenon is quite real, quite objective, but the *cause* is rooted in some peculiar mental talent — perhaps of one of its apparent victims.

7

The Hatter's Castle

Freud was not the first to suspect hidden currents of the mind, but he might as well have been. His experience of hypnosis and hysteria led him to draw a map with two main zones. One was the conscious mind, which we all know about. The other was the subconscious, which is usually hidden.

Freud imagined the subconscious to be a sort of rubbish dump, the place where the mind discards old thoughts, memories and feelings. It was also the home of primitive urges like the sex drive; and in some cases it was the cause of troublesome behaviour patterns.

One of Freud's most brilliant pupils was a Swiss named Carl Jung, who came to view the mind rather differently. Jung did not accept the central position of sexuality in human behaviour. He believed the mind had hidden depths and interesting talents. Nor was he convinced that the theory of the subconscious proposed by Freud explained everything that was in there. He developed his own theory of a 'collective unconscious' common to all humanity and peopled it with 'entities' which he called 'archetypes'.

The term 'entities' is in inverted commas — but only just. Jung defined an archetype as a pre-existent psychic constellation of ideas and attitudes with a predictable behaviour pattern. But he considered archetypes, like the collective unconscious itself, to be subjective *and objective* at the same time.

This is a difficult concept to follow and Jung's academic style does not make it any easier. Attempts to resolve the paradox led to a picture of the archetypes as immaterial personalities —

something suspiciously like ghosts, or what the ancients thought of as 'the gods'. Jung was well aware of this interpretation and seemed untroubled by it. Freud, by contrast, had a horror of 'the dark tide of the occult' and rejected such concepts completely. The differences of opinion became the cause of serious conflict between the two psychiatrists.

One of the most bitter areas of this conflict was the fact that Jung remained convinced some mental contents could 'exteriorize' — that is to say, could make themselves directly felt in the outside world. A frequently quoted story tells of a discussion on this point between Jung and Freud. Jung felt a burning sensation in the pit of his stomach, directly followed by a loud crack from a nearby sideboard.

'There, Herr Professor,' Jung exclaimed. 'That is an example of an exteriorization phenomenon. Furthermore, I predict that the sound will immediately occur again!' And it did, much to Freud's discomfort.

It is easy to forget that the whole science of psychology is an attempt to find explanations for things psychologists *observe*. While psychological experiments are frequently carried out, it is not an experimental science in the sense that, for example, chemistry is an experimental science. The object of psychological study — the human mind — is beyond the reach of science. It cannot be weighed, dissected or measured. It cannot even really be given a location in space. In psychology, there are no absolute answers — only theories. If a man exhibits peculiarities in his behaviour, he may be suffering from a psychosis. But the theory of psychosis is fashionable rather than proven. In another age, the same patient might have been thought to be possessed by an evil spirit. It is difficult to prove this theory too, but it does underline the fact that there are no certainties in mental matters. Freud did not believe the mind could exert a direct influence on the world; Jung did. Either could be correct, but the weight of subsequent evidence has certainly fallen on the side of Jung.

Jung's ideas, like those of his mentor, were largely formulated during the Victorian era at about the time when a minority of scientists were just beginning to take a serious experimental interest in the paranormal. Oddly enough, the two streams of thought remained largely separate until the early 1930s when an American scientist, Dr J. B. Rhine of the University of North Carolina suddenly combined the two.

Until Rhine's experiments began, there had been a tendency to lump things like telepathy, levitation, clairvoyance, precognition and psychokinesis in the same occult ragbag as ghosts, ghouls, vampires, werewolves and demons. Rhine took the unusual step (for a scientist) of dipping into this ragbag. And if he left the werewolves, ghosts and vampires severely alone, he did pull out something almost as controversial — telepathy.

Until then, telepathy had been left to philosophers and those psychical researchers who sometimes speculated on it as a sideline to their main task of investigating mediums and psychics. Rhine, however, considered there might well be something in it. He was at least prepared to put it to the experimental test.

To do this, he devised a series of card-calling experiments. The cards used were specially designed — a pack of twenty-five showing various emotionally neutral symbols like a square, a circle or a set of wavy lines. This Zener pack, as it was called, proved necessary because a noticeable number of subjects unconsciously fought shy of naming certain cards in a normal pack. The Ace of Spades, for example, is widely thought of as unlucky — a death card. The avoidance of cards for emotional reasons wrecked the statistical basis of Rhine's experiments, so he dropped the use of the normal pack completely.

With the Zener pack, however, he was able to have subjects guess at what card was being drawn and studied. The guesses were noted and the number correct out of a given run subjected to probability analysis. Probability analysis can get complicated: it involves some hefty mathematical formulae. But the principle is simple enough. If you are asked to guess which of five different cards I happen to be looking at, the laws of chance give you 5 to 1 odds against your being right. Another way of looking at this is that if you were to take *five* guesses, sheer luck would let you get one right over the run.

But things become interesting when you consistently guess

better than sheer luck allows. Over longish runs, the deviation from chance expectation can be analysed and probability calculus applied to show the odds against the possibility that, however many you guessed right, you were really only pushing your luck.

This, in essence, is what Rhine did. After a time, he discovered that the odds against luck in the guesses of his star subjects ran into tens of thousands to one. He concluded he had established a statistical basis for the reality of telepathy.

During the time this was going on, a young gambler suggested Rhine might like to test the belief — quite common amongst gamblers — that when he had a certain feeling (got 'hot', as he expressed it) he was able to influence the roll of the dice.

Intrigued by the notion, Rhine introduced dice-throwing into his experiments. Probability analysis showed the results to be statistically significant: PK seemed to be a factor in the experiments — or at least *something* was causing the dice to fall in a way that could not be attributed purely to chance. Other researchers subsequently carried out similar experiments using Rhine's procedure or their own modifications of it. The results were confirmed.

But it was a *statistical* confirmation only. When subjects tried to roll a six, then six came up a little more often than the mathematics of probability said it should. But no one was able to keep rolling sixes at will. PK ability gave a gambler an edge, but it was a small edge and nobody could ever be sure when it would come up in time to save his shirt.

Early on in these experiments, some curious findings emerged. One was that the *amount* of physical matter involved did not affect the appearance of PK — at least not in the way one might expect. Many subjects showed conclusively that they performed better when two dice were used, rather than one. As Rhine has pointed out, common sense would tell you that it should be twice as hard to influence two dice. But this was not the case.

For some time, scientific attention was directed towards refining the test procedure, making it increasingly foolproof. But when the PK factor continued to appear, the thrust of effort gradually turned towards determining what exactly the power was.

Here the early two-dice preference suddenly became important. The most obvious theory to explain PK was that the subjects were using some sort of energy to influence matter. Indeed, careful measurements suggested an unknown energy was present. But it was an energy which refused to behave itself. It did not work in the same way as any other energy known to physics. Generally speaking, the amount of energy required to move a physical object increases with the mass of that object: you need more muscle to lift a heavy weight than a light one.

PK energy, by contrast, treated all tested amounts of mass as if they were exactly the same. This was actually demonstrated right down to electron level. Whatever the mass, whatever the material, if PK energy was present, it could be shifted — at least, this was *almost* the situation.

Two other factors quickly emerged. The first was that while mass made no difference in the range where PK worked, PK would not work at all once the object went above a certain size. In this sense, mass appeared to be extremely important.

This is a little confusing, but all it means is that as long as PK subjects worked on objects below a certain mass, the PK energy produced results to exactly the same degree whatever the amount of mass present. But once you introduced an object *above* a certain size (mass) PK stopped working altogether.

The second factor was that the dividing line was neither constant nor absolute. That is to say, one subject might not be able to tackle an object because of its size, while another handled it with ease. Worse still, there were some *materials* which certain subjects could not influence, irrespective of the fact that they had successfully influenced similar objects of identical mass made from different materials.

If all this is beginning to sound technical, I'm afraid it is going to get worse before it gets better. The question of preference became even more convoluted when it was discovered that subjects actually showed a *negative* PK ability when faced with materials they did not like. Lead dice, for example, proved very unpopular. Subjects using them could cause their target number to arise *fewer* times than could be accounted for by chance. They were using their PK ability to miss the target rather than hit it. To the lay person, negative PK seems very odd — perhaps even faintly ridiculous. To the scientist, it is just as evidential as its positive manifestation.

However, the evidence generated by the Rhine style of experiment indicated the existence of PK only in very limited degrees. Subjects might prove they could (sometimes!) influence the roll of a die. None of them ever managed to make the die roll of its own accord.

Rhine's experiments were well conceived. There were criticisms of his early structures, but he was quick to improve his methods and his most important work is beyond criticism on technical grounds. This did not, of course, prevent criticism arising. A majority of scientists were unwilling to face the implications of something like telepathy. Freud was not the only one with a horror of the dark tide of the occult.

In these circumstances, it is not surprising to learn that reactions in the scientific community to what was going on in North Carolina varied. A few — a very few — scientists showed unbiased interest in the work and made their own attempts to duplicate his findings. A larger number attacked the experiments and occasionally the reputation of the experimenter. The majority simply ignored them.

Part of the problem was the difficulty we mentioned earlier in relation to psychology: Rhine was attempting to study something which could not be weighed and measured. Scientists, like stevedores, are earthy people. They like to deal with things they can touch. While the maverick Rhine was playing cards to learn about the phantom mind, another less controversial school of experimenters were approaching the whole thing from an altogether more respectable direction. They were messing around with the brain.

Nobody seriously doubts that brain and mind are closely linked. It has even been argued that the mind does not exist in its own right — that it is actually only our experience of brain activity. But even those who do not go this far have to admit the brain is a fascinating organ.

Since the days of Broca, one of the first scientists to devote a career to its examination, the human brain has gradually yielded up more and more of its secrets. It carries the clear stamp of its own evolution in its structure. Inside your skull is a small reptilian knob at the end of the spine. This is overlaid by a second, mammalian brain: and finally by that third area of grey matter which makes you uniquely human.

Effects of brain surgery on behaviour have long been noted. Even a small incision in the wrong place can turn a person into a vegetable. But in the twentieth century, brain investigators gradually abandoned the scalpel for an instrument of much greater precision – the electrode. If the brain is a machine, it is an electrical machine and small currents through fine wires in carefully defined areas can produce remarkable disruptions in its function.

Some of these disruptions have a clear bearing on the mystery of the mind. Electrical stimulus can produce vivid hallucinations or cause patients to relive past experiences in total detail. It has even been shown that a particular probe will create that curious feeling of *déjàvu*, the sensation of having been here before that occultists sometimes link with the theory of reincarnation.

Interesting though they were, these findings caused far less of a stir than a more recent discovery that the brain may be divided into two halves, each of which has its own distinct set of functions. The breakthrough here was made largely by accident. Normally the halves are connected by a tissue bridge. If you leave this bridge alone, everything functions normally. And even if you cut the connection, everything *seems* to function normally. Severing the bridge was once thought of as a promising treatment for epilepsy: it prevents the disease spreading. Patients so treated showed little apparent sign that anything was amiss: but this was because the changes were subtle.

In point of fact, it was careful examination of such patients which led science to the discovery of a sort of dual personality in each of us: the rational and the creative, the verbal and the visual, the thinking and the feeling, different but complementary so long as the tissue bridge remains intact. It is as if you were actually two people, living in fairly close co-operation and so accustomed to the situation that they had long convinced themselves they were actually one. In right-handed people the creative half of this curious partnership 'lives' in the right brain, and the rational in the left.

Research in this whole area is still continuing, but already some fascinating discoveries have emerged. Your self-awareness seems to be almost totally confined to the part of you that lives in the left brain. Just next door, however, there is a stranger with considerable talents. Split brain patients have shown us a physical basis for Freud's two fold division of the human psyche into the conscious and the unconscious. For conscious read left brain; for unconscious read right.

The $64,000 question is, of course, just what abilities does the mysterious right brain possess? Who really lives in this hatter's castle?

8

Moving Molehills

Rhine's initial statistical experiments were conducted in the early 1930s. It was several decades later before reports began to filter through about scientific investigation into an altogether more spectacular form of PK. These reports emerged from behind the Iron Curtain.

According to the stories, Russian scientists had captured a rare bird: someone who could, under test conditions, actually make things move by mindpower. And the influence was not merely statistical. Inanimate objects actually shifted discernibly and measurably. The process could be observed, could — and had — been filmed.

The focus of all the scientific attention was a remarkable Muscovite named, in the early reports, as Nelya Mikhailova. It subsequently transpired that this name was false (the woman in question was actually called Nina Kulagina) but the remainder of the reports were all too true. In Madame Kulagina, the Russians had discovered a genuine PK medium, someone with the conscious, controlled and repeatable ability to think objects into motion.

The objects themselves were not terribly large. Madame Kulagina could spin a compass needle or persuade a cigarette to crawl across the table: and on one delightful occasion she caused a journalist's sandwich to jump right off his plate.

But the effort involved in these effects was frightening. In a typical PK session, Madame Kulagina would lose literally pounds in weight over a matter of hours. Her heart rate soared to three and four times its norm. She ended experiments bathed in sweat and totally exhausted. After one prolonged series of experiments, she actually had to be hospitalized.

With Nina Kulagina, we move to the very heart of our present thesis. Repeatedly, under the most stringent test conditions, she proved conclusively that the human mind can exert a direct influence on physical matter: or at very least direct some unknown and undetected form of energy to do the same job.

In science there is a useful principle known as Occam's Razor. It states that when you are presented with a mystery, you are not entitled to insist on a complicated explanation if a simple one will do. Nor do you need to look for a new (unproven) theory when a tested idea fits the facts equally well.

By using Occam's Razor, it is possible at this stage to cut at least a thin slice off the poltergeist mystery. When you forget all preconceived ideas, poltergeist phenomena involve physical objects moving about of their own accord. It is easy to assume the cause is a ghost. But while people have believed in ghosts for centuries, the entities have never been subjected to laboratory analysis. Thus, ghosts as an explanation of poltergeist phenomena, fall into the category of an unproven theory. Even if ghosts exist, we do not know that they are capable of moving objects around.

The alternative theory of poltergeist phenomena suggests that the objects are actually thrown around by some nearby human mind. The fact that the person who owns the mind knows nothing about it need not trouble us. Both Freud and the split brain scientists have shown we are not always aware of what our minds are doing. The only question that remains is whether or not human minds are *capable* of influencing matter in this way. Rhine showed that they are, to a very limited degree. Madame Kulagina showed that they are as well; and in a far more spectacular manner.

But the contrast between the effort needed to produce minor PK effects in the laboratory and the ease with which poltergeists produce much larger effects, is striking. And if poltergeists are actually human minds working at an unconscious level, why the enormous difference?

There is no easy answer to this question, but investigators continued to refine the theory since it seemed to fit so many of the facts. Perhaps inevitably, sex raised its head. The suggestion was made that the energy which drove gross (poltergeist) PK was sexual in nature. In adolescence, massive glandular changes typically produce emotional turmoil – the reason why so many teenagers are impossible to live with – and the sex drive reaches a higher level than at any other time. Add to this the very genuine frustrations teenagers face in various aspects of their lives and, argued the scientists, the inner pressures might well exteriorize – another way of saying poltergeist effects might manifest.

This proved a very interesting theory so far as it went; and in many cases it seemed sufficient to provide a reasonable explanation of what was happening. But it did not explain all cases. And in no case did it give any real hint of the *mechanism* by which emotional turmoil suddenly began to throw chairs around the room.

There was, however, a promising line of investigation apparent in certain cases. Poltergeist effects were not entirely random. In the Bell case, for example, John Bell was very systematically persecuted. In many another case, the more attention was given to the poltergeist, the more antics it got up to. Then too, there was the matter of poltergeist *suggestibility*. It is suggested that the 'ghost' might bring in some wood and the ghost does so. It is hoped (aloud) that the poltergeist will not break a window, and the window is promptly broken.

Hypnotists are familiar with this phenomenon: an entranced subject is equally suggestible. But in the case of hypnosis, the hypnotist is making suggestions directly to the subject's unconscious mind. The conscious mind is temporarily in abeyance. By analogy, it seemed that poltergeist 'carriers' might be individuals whose unconscious minds began to reach out into the physical world to produce startling effects. In doing so, the unconscious was seeking its own gratifications (quite unsuspected by the individuals concerned). These gratifications might be no more than a desire for attention, for a feeling of importance or an urge to power. Or they might be the persecution of a despised parent, untouchable in any other way.

But the unconscious was still the unconscious, still subject to its own laws. And one of those laws seems to be that when the unconscious is exposed, be it through hypnosis or poltergeist manifestation, it becomes susceptible to suggestion. Thus, in superstitious times, 'poltergeists' (i.e. the unconscious minds of the carriers) were suggested into believing themselves devils, while our own Space Age has produced the odd poltergeist which believes itself to be a Martian.

The more attention was paid to this idea, the more reasonable it sounded. But still the fundamental mechanism eluded the investigators. PK under conscious control moved molehills at best. Unconscious PK, by contrast, seemed almost able to move mountains. Why the difference?

Science, frankly, has not yet come up with any answer. But the idea of explaining poltergeists as mindpower now seems so promising that we are fully entitled to accept it as a working hypothesis and cast around for other facts which might fit the developing picture. Some of these facts can only be found in unfamiliar places.

Madame Alexandra David-Neel remains to this day the only European woman ever to have been honoured with the rank of Lama. During a long and eventful life, she travelled extensively throughout Tibet, studying its curious customs. Personal interest encouraged her to concentrate on age-old Tibetan religious and mystical practices.

Several of these practices — which flourished widely before the Chinese Communists clamped down on native Tibetan Buddhism — were extremely bizarre to Western eyes. Perhaps the most bizarre of all was that which involved the *Yidam*.

A Yidam, according to Tibetan Buddhist doctrine, is a fearsome deity, half god, half demon, yet somehow associated with teaching. The old books of Tibet carried pictures of such creatures, drawn — and often coloured — by generations of patient monks.

But Madame David-Neel discovered that the Yidam was something more than the Oriental equivalent of Europe's dead-letter medieval demonology. To initiated Lamas, the Yidam was a reality with a very special purpose.

In order to understand this purpose, it is necessary first to understand something of the ancient culture of Tibet. The country was, prior to the early 1950s, a medieval theocracy ruled over by a god-king, the Dalai Lama. Religion permeated every facet of Tibetan life. One man in every four — 25 per cent of the total male population — was a monk. Religion was the country's largest industry.

Within the monasteries, some of which were actually small towns, monks carried on a tradition of mystical practice that dated back for centuries and included doctrines about the nature and structure of the human mind which remain virtually unrecognized in Europe. Yet those few Westerners who have taken the trouble to study them (like the psychologist Carl Jung) tend to agree that they contain some startling insights into human psychology.

Methods of religious instruction in Tibet were essentially similar to such methods anywhere: students studied scriptures, listened to lectures and memorized doctrines. But there was also a *practical* aspect to the study for those who cared to undertake it. This aspect involved techniques seldom, if ever, seen in the West. Among these techniques was the use of the Yidam.

Typically, a *chela* or pupil would bind himself to a single Adept in a one-to-one relationship in which orders were carried out without question. The pupil's training might include various trance induction methods and such useful yoga practices as that of *tumo* which generates a high degree of body heat. But sooner or later, the pupil would be required to meditate on his tutelary deity, the Yidam.

The meditation was usually carried out in strict seclusion, aided by images of the deity. The pupil was required to build a picture in his own imagination. This was reinforced by such rituals as the drawing of a *kyilkhor* — a sort of magic circle made from multicoloured chalks. This stage of the process might go on for months, or even years. The end result was supposed to be the appearance to the pupil of the Yidam itself.

It should be noted that to the average Tibetan, gods and demons were a literal reality, inhabitants of a spirit world who could, under certain circumstances, invade this one. Since the meditation regime allowed the pupil little time to eat or sleep, it is scarcely surprising that, given time, the Yidam did indeed seem to appear — usually briefly, when the pupil was close to exhaustion.

In the West, we would, of course, explain this as hallucination. The Tibetans, both Adept and pupil, took a different view. When the vision was reported back, the Adept would encourage the pupil to continue with his exercises with renewed enthusiasm in order to persuade the fleeting Yidam to remain for a longer time.

If the pupil did so, the time would inevitably come when the 'hallucination' became permanent. So far as the pupil was concerned, the Yidam was always within the magic circle of the kyilkhor. But this would not be quite good enough for his teacher. Further meditations were urged until the pupil could actually feel the Yidam's touch; and finally until this mentally constructed creature could be persuaded to leave the circle and accompany the pupil wherever he went.

The picture that springs to Western minds is that of young men driven over the brink of insanity. But is this really the case?

A parallel, if somewhat less difficult, Tibetan mystical technique was that of *tulpa creation*. Here, no specific deity or demon was involved. The pupil was only required to develop his powers of concentration until he could visualize something so strongly that it appeared to take on objective reality. The thing visualized was called a *tulpa* and it might take almost any form.

Madame David-Neel became intrigued by the technique of tulpa creation and decided to try it out for herself. The tulpa she chose was whimsical — a plump, bald, brown-robed monk, not unlike Friar Tuck. Over a period of months, she concentrated on this image as often as circumstances allowed and was eventually rewarded by its apparently objective appearance.

So far, nothing more mysterious was going on than a woman seeing what she wanted to see — the same sort of trained hallucination as in the case of the Yidam. But then other members of her party began to enquire who the brown-robed monk was.

It seemed that this 'hallucination' was perceptible to others as well as Madame David-Neel.

Worse was to come. The day arrived when the tulpa showed up without Madame David-Neel willing it. Thereafter, it appeared quite frequently of its own accord. Furthermore, its appearance underwent a subtle change, growing slimmer and more sinister. Complaints from the travel party became frequent: a number of the native Tibetans were increasingly fearful of the stranger in their midst. Madame David-Neel eventually had to 'absorb' her creation (how, she does not tell us but apparently the job caused her considerable difficulty).

The report of Madame David-Neel's tulpa is similar in many respects to the equally unusual case reported by Violet Firth, the British psychic and occultist who wrote under the pen-name Dion Fortune. Ms Firth awoke one morning to discover an 'astral wolf' at the foot of her bed. As a student of Freudian analysis as well as the occult, she concluded this was an aspect of her own unconscious mind that had somehow 'exteriorized' in the night. She too had to absorb the phantom, again with considerable difficulty.

Can concentration (or some curious natural talent like that of Dion Fortune) really produce exteriorized creations of the mind which have all the hallmarks of a ghost? Tibet is far away and there are those who find the reports of occultists notoriously unreliable. Yet in the early 1970s, something happened which put the question beyond all reasonable doubt. It happened not in Asia, but in Canada. And it happened not to mystics, but to scientists.

A group of investigators from the Toronto Society for Psychical Research, under the leadership of Dr George and Mrs Iris Owen decided to attempt one of the most remarkable experiments in the entire history of their speciality. They set out to *make* a ghost.

The method they used bears certain similarities to the Tibetan techniques of Yidam calling and tulpa creation. First, in the manner of a fiction writer, they created a character, then invented a background and life to go with him.

The group's character, Philip, would have done full justice to any historical thriller. It was decided he had lived in the time of Cromwell, in a house called Diddington Manor. As part of the overall life story, Philip fell in love with a beautiful gypsy woman named Margo and subsequently had an affair with her. Dorothea, Philip's wife, found out about the relationship and took her revenge by accusing Margo of witchcraft. Margo was tried, convicted and burned at the stake. Philip, mad with grief, committed suicide by throwing himself off the battlements of his home.

It must be stressed that all of this was fiction, with one sole exception: there actually was a Diddington Manor, pictures of which had been obtained by the group. But no one named Philip had ever lived there, nor did Margo or the jealous Dorothea ever exist.

Having formulated this tale, the group then tried to bring Philip to life (so to speak) by means of a series of seances. Photographs of the manor were placed around the seance room and the group met regularly to concentrate on the fictional Philip and his dramatic life story.

For several months nothing happened. It seemed as if the experiment was to be a failure. Then the group decided on a different approach. The intensive concentration was abandoned in favour of a much more informal atmosphere. The group chatted about Philip and their experiment. At one point they even sang a few songs!

Surprisingly, this latter approach proved productive. At one seance, a rap was heard. The group promptly set up a code and communication was established with the 'spirit'. And sure enough, the 'spirit' was Philip, claiming the life history they had invented for him.

The phenomena increased in strength until Philip was able to make the seance room table move. (It is even reported that, at a public demonstration, the table danced up the steps onto the platform of its own accord! An exaggeration, perhaps, but one which still indicates the direction events were taking.)

Stranger still was to come. During a lengthy series of communications, Philip gave so many circumstantial details of the Cromwellian period that group members began to wonder if they had really invented the ghost, or somehow managed to draw up the life story of someone who had actually lived. This is less outlandish than it might sound, as most psychologists — and quite a few professional authors — will confirm. A snippet of information read years ago will often surface in the mind, apparently as fiction, but actually as an unconscious recollection of fact. But further investigation in this case still failed to give Philip the slightest historical validity. The character was fictional, the 'ghost' a creation of the group.

But as a creation of the group, Philip somehow managed to give out far more than had originally been put into him. He was able to relate detail after detail of his period, far and beyond anything consciously included in the fictional life story. Even more amazingly, he would occasionally come up with information *unknown to group members at the time.* Such information, when checked against written sources later, proved to be historically accurate.

Fascinating though all this may be, the major import to our present thesis is the fact that Philip made the table move. In Philip, we have a 'poltergeist' with the poltergeist's normal ability to move objects. Yet Philip himself was the creation of a group of human minds, not the spirit of some long-dead personality.

Here at last we have the missing link between poltergeist and PK. It is a link we shall be developing much further in the course of this book, for it suggests that poltergeists, far from being the mischievous 'ghosts' or 'spirits' which humanity has so long assumed them to be, are in fact, something very different: creations of the human mind — but creations which make use of powers only half suspected by the scientific establishment.

What we are talking about here, in both poltergeist cases and Spiritualist seances, is the possibility of participants unwittingly producing phenomena which, while their own creation, is nonetheless quite objective. It is vitally important to realize that in this context we are not speaking of hallucination or imagination. Even if we allow that the entities are artificial in the sense that they are actually created by participants, they can nonetheless produce objective noises (raps) like Philip and might, as a product of PK, even materialize.

This point becomes especially important when we come to deal with gross PK generated by experimental groups. Such groups may begin by moving tables, but a whole range of physical phenomena — and the possible appearance of a 'guiding intelligence' — can and usually do arise eventually — all created by the group and all totally objective.

9

Poltergeists by the Tail

A do-it-yourself ghost is such an intrinsically fascinating project that it is not surprising to learn of several groups which followed the Toronto example. Despite difficulties and a touch of whimsy (one group created a phantom talking dolphin named Silk) very positive results were obtained, including some reported table levitations. In 1977, one published source suggested that the fictional Philip had actually manifested as a 'Raudive voice'.

This was an exceptionally interesting development. The late Dr Konstantin Raudive was a Latvian psychologist with a considerable scientific interest in the paranormal. Following on some experiments carried out in Scandinavia, he discovered that he could pick up mysterious fragments of speech using an ordinary tape recorder attached to a simple diode.

These 'Raudive voices' as they came to be called, spoke in a daunting variety of different languages — frequently in the same sentence — and claimed to be communicating spirits of the dead.

Some of the most sceptical electronic engineers in Europe examined Raudive's tapes with, so far as I am aware, universal agreement that they were genuine — at least to the extent that the voices had left actual traces on the magnetic tape and that there was no rational explanation for them.

Since the communicating 'entities' included many famous names — John F. Kennedy, Sir Winston Churchill and Adolf Hitler among them — the phenomenon attracted a great deal of attention. The experiments were successfully repeated by others under the most stringent test conditions and yet more voices produced, without, however, the multi-lingual quality which characterized those produced by Raudive himself.

In public, Dr Raudive maintained a detached posture, generally claiming only that here was a phenomenon which warranted investigation. Privately he seems to have been convinced that the voices were what they claimed to be: communications from beyond the grave. During our brief correspondence before his death, he also suggested there was a mediumistic aspect to the phenomenon. This was something which had been long suspected by others working in the field. It was thought significant that Raudive, who was an exceptional linguist, produced multi-lingual voices, while others less talented in languages did not.

During a television forum on the subject, I put forward the suggestion that the voices might actually result from a direct influence on the tape by the mind of the experimenter. I was thinking at the time of the American, Ted Serios, who had shown, more or less conclusively, that he was capable of imprinting mental images on Polaroid film. My notion received scant support: the consensus of the forum believed, with Raudive, that the voices were post mortem communications. Now it appears that mindpower must be given more serious consideration as an explanation for at least some of the voices.

So much interesting material has arisen out of the Toronto experiment that it is important to examine the methods used to bring it about. The creation of a fictional character was ingenious and quite obviously central to the project, but it was not enough to guarantee success. In the last chapter I mentioned briefly that several months went by without any manifestations worth noting. In fact, the group met weekly for the better part of a year before a radical change of method produced dramatic results.

At first they treated the experiment with commendable seriousness. Their approach was one of quietly meditating on the character of Philip and attempting, a little like the Tibetan chela, to produce a sort of group hallucination. When nothing much happened and patience was (presumably) wearing thin, they switched to a much more relaxed approach. Chatting and jokes were no longer taboo and at one stage they even took to singing songs. It was in the course of this delightful eccentricity that Philip chose to rap for the first time.

This new, informal approach (adopted in 1973) was not, perhaps, arbitrarily chosen. It had been used, with considerable success in a slightly different context, in Britain since the middle 1960s. The man who developed it was a psychologist named Kenneth Batcheldor.

One of the earliest indications that something new and exciting was going on in the world of paranormal investigations came with the publication, in the Journal of the Society for Psychical Research dated September 1966, of a drily titled 'Report on a Case of Table Levitation and Associated Phenomena' by K. J. Batcheldor.

But if the title was dry, the content was not. The punch came in the very first paragraph of the Introduction. After making the point that a major difficulty in the study of psychical phenomena was the rarity of their occurrence, Batcheldor dropped his bombshell with the words: 'As the writer has had the good fortune to witness and experiment on total levitation of tables and allied phenomena, he offers here an account of his experiences.'

This quietly confident assertion was a bombshell indeed. Historical references to levitation abound – generally associated with saints or mystics – but time has placed them beyond legitimate scientific investigation. Victorian Spiritualism laid claim to levitations, both of people – like the medium D. D. Home, who was once seen to float out through one upstairs window and in another – and of furniture. This *was* often investigated by scientists of the day, but their technology was limited and their methodology not always strict.

And since the first frantic wave of Spiritualism died down, spectacular phenomena like table-turning sank gradually into abeyance. As Batcheldor remarked, a major obstacle to the study of this type of phenomena had become the rarity of its occurrence.

Now, however, it seemed the situation was about to change. The Journal report described a series of 200 experimental sittings which began on 25 April 1964. Regular sitters were named only as Batcheldor himself, Miss P. M. Coghlan and Mr W. G. Chick. Others did take part — family and friends, as they are referred to in the report — but only for a comparatively few sittings.

Of the 200 experiments, 120 produced virtually no results. Batcheldor notes that Chick was absent from all these: he had become half convinced that Chick was a medium, although later he abandoned this theory for a more developed thesis of group action. Whatever the reason, 70 out of the 80 sittings at which Chick *did* attend produced phenomena. It was these 'positive' sittings which formed the basis of the report.

Batcheldor states bluntly that neither he nor his fellow sitters had any experience of table levitation prior to the experiments. Nor, despite the suspicions about Chick, did they lay claim to mediumistic powers. Indeed, the first few sessions seem to have been in the nature of an entertainment, the sort of parlour game investigation most intelligent individuals get up to at some time of their lives.

There *were* some examples of table movement in these early sessions, but nothing that could not be accounted for by involuntary muscle action. Then, on the eleventh sitting (and to the expressed shock of Batcheldor) the table rose clear off the floor and floated in the air. In that instant, any question of involuntary muscle action was dramatically ruled out.

'It seemed,' wrote Batcheldor, 'that we had stumbled on a genuinely paranormal force.'

The group agreed to continue with the sittings to find out what it was. They also tightened their experimental procedures considerably. Over a series of 200 sittings, running through until December 1965, some 800 pages of written notes were generated and of the 70 sittings with positive results, 27 of these were tape-recorded.

Such procedures are vitally necessary in an area where human memory is notoriously fallible. But human observation is equally unreliable. The first complete levitation occurred in total darkness and was determined only by the feel of the table and the sound it made falling back onto the floor. Batcheldor remarks that this is not quite so unreliable as it seems, since by the time it happened the group had considerable experience. But he was aware there was considerable room for improvement if the experiments were to be accepted as valid, and so he cast about for some instrument which would detect table movement.

In the event, he manufactured his own device. Each table foot was connected to a simple pressure switch and joined to a small, battery-operated bulb set in the centre of the table. The switches were such that the lamp would only light when all four feet were simultaneously off the floor.

This worked well enough, but Batcheldor remained dissatisfied. There was a possibility that the lighting of the lamp might be no more than a collective hallucination. Although unlikely, it was a loophole in the procedure which needed to be closed. This was duly done by replacing the lamp with a buzzer, the difference being that the sound of the buzzer could be tape-recorded.

A minor hitch remained. In the course of the experiments it was discovered that the switch would operate if the table tilted more than 40 degrees. While this resulted in a false levitation signal, it made little practical difference to the experiments since it was always possible to determine when a large tilt took place.

Nonetheless, further safeguards were added in the form of photographs. These included stereoscopic pictures and used normal, electronic and infra-red flash. At the time Batcheldor published his original report, no really evidential photographs were produced. The best showed a tilt with one of those present actually sitting on the table, but no picture emerged of total levitation. (This situation changed later, as we shall see, but in these experiments failures proved as important as successes in developing Batcheldor's current theory of gross PK.)

At the time, Batcheldor did no more than note the major difficulties with photography: it was disruptive for some of the sitters, it was physically difficult to keep a camera properly trained on a table which tended to skeeter all around the room, and *levitations were considerably less frequent once photographic apparatus was set up.* This last point was to prove far more important than it sounds.

Various other measures were introduced in the hope of catching PK force by the tail. Sitters were weighed, for example, during table movements; and at least one of them endured an experiment in which his legs were encased in a large plastic bag. To the group it was obvious that something was going on and Batcheldor was determined to discover exactly what it was. Sessions were held under different lighting conditions – from daylight to total darkness. It was quickly discovered that darkness was best, although gradually levitations began to occur under the dim glow of a photographic safety light.

In his account, Batcheldor gave a fascinating insight into these early sessions by describing a typical successful sitting thus:

A typical sitting lasted about two hours, which just filled a 7-inch spool of standard-play recording tape at 3¾ inches per second. There was usually a break of half an hour at half-time.

At the commencement, the sitters took their places at a table in the centre of an ordinary living room containing other furniture. The tape-recorder and special light (if any) were switched on, and the main lights off.

Hands were placed palms down on the upper surface of the table. Except for special experiments no attempt was made to touch fingers or link into a circle as some others have done. The attitude we adopted was one of enquiry, with no attempt to create a religious atmosphere as in Spiritualism. No prayers, hymns or music formed part of the conditions (except that on one occasion the table spelled out 'Musick' and we obliged with a song). No restriction was placed on conversation, which sometimes became animated. No one went into trance.

There was always an initial period of waiting before anything happened. This wait was usually 5-10 min., though it could be as short as 1 min. or as long as half an hour. A quick start usually foretold a good session, but a slow start was not necessarily a bad sign: in some cases a slow start was followed by paucity of phenomena but in other cases phenomena picked up well in the second half.

The first signs of activity were usually creaks or cracking noises in the wood of the table. Most of these seemed normally producible by sideways stress on the table and may be called crepitations. But these were interspersed with sharp taps, scrapings or soft thuds, apparently due to some separate body striking the table.

In a few instances, the latter noises were unmistakably heard on our chairs, on the floor or on the walls.

After a few minutes of these noises, the table usually performed two or three 'slides' at intervals: that is to say it slid along the floor for a few inches.

After a further pause, the table would tilt up on two legs then drop again. Tilts and slides would then continue at intervals, often interspersed with crepitations and raps.

The simple motions of sliding and tilting were capable of enormous variation: the table could glide slowly and silently as if on candle grease, or make a rapid and noisy excursion of six feet or more, causing the sitters to leave their seats and stumble after it. It could tilt with extreme slowness or extreme rapidity, and descend in complete silence or with such a crash that we feared it would go right through the floorboards. It could beat an enormous tattoo, quite disturbing to the neighbours when the table weighed 40 lb! Sometimes it would rotate about its centre, either slowly, or so nearly instantaneously as to take the breath away.

Even these movements, short of total levitations, were hard to explain on the theory of unconscious muscular action: in fact, far from helping the movements, we found it next to impossible to stop them by bearing down on the table or sitting on it.

As the sitting proceeded, the movements of the table usually increased in power and extent. Under these circumstances it was often impossible to remain seated, and the chairs were pushed back and we continued standing. Sometimes we had to go at a brisk pace from one end of the room to the other, even with a heavy (40 lb) table.

On many occasions (more frequently in earlier meetings) the table was totally levitated, sometimes remaining suspended in the air for twenty seconds (15 lb table, timed with stopwatch from recorded buzzer).

When the power had built up, various experiments were tried for the remainder of the sitting. Sometimes we took our hands off and watched the table moving without contact . . . In most sittings, attempts were made to communicate with any directing intelligence, occasionally with considerable response, but more often than not with no response: in our series of sittings, the 'messages' which usually figure so prominently in table-tilting were few and far between.

Other spontaneous phenomena which could occur in a sitting were: breezes, intense cold, lights, touchings, pulling back of sitters' chairs, movement of objects (rattle, trumpet), 'gluing' of the table to the floor so that it could not be budged, and 'apports'.

The description is, of course, a composite. Phenomena varied enormously from sitting to sitting. In the very first meeting, for example, nothing at all happened except for minor vibrations of the table which could easily have been caused by unconscious muscular tremors. By the eleventh session, however, matters had developed to such a degree that the first total levitation occurred.

'The table (15 lb) rose an inch or so and swayed from side to side four times with the motion of a pendulum,' Batcheldor wrote. 'We had no check on this except our sense of touch and the fact that it was silent: noise recommenced when the table scraped back into contact with the floor. There was also the fact that a pendulum motion could not have been produced by pushing, since pushing causes either a straight slide or a turning about the lower extremities of the table.'

Batcheldor and his colleagues found the total levitation 'fascinating but disconcerting' and in the days that followed began to wonder if they might not have fallen victim to illusion. In order to be sure, their next meeting began with the 15 lb table equipped with the lamp and switchpads on the feet.

The session proved rewarding. At first the lamp lit only briefly, indicating a short total levitation, but then the movements grew bolder and the lamp remained lit for longer periods.

> By its red glow we could clearly see our hands on top of the table. The table then seemed to act as an excited person would and proceeded to execute all manner of very lively movements – rocking, swaying, jumping, dancing, tilting, oscillating bodily both slowly and rapidly: it shook like a live thing even when totally levitated, almost shaking our hands off. Because the levitations were not very high, I said: 'Come on – higher!' at which the table rose up chest high and remained there for eight seconds.

Dramatic though this sounds, the phenomena actually grew stronger. Batcheldor went on to report that at one point the table lifted five inches off the floor, floated across the room so that the group had to leave their seats to follow it, then crashed into some other furniture against the wall. This was followed by a period in which the table rose up and crashed down with such force that the sitters feared it would break.

Overall, this session produced more total levitations than any other of the series. One sitter counted eighty-four.

Against this background, it is not surprising that the group approached their next meeting convinced anything could happen. Curiously, for the first hour, absolutely nothing did. Then, during the second half of the sitting, the table took to making sudden, startling darting movements, separated by long pauses. Batcheldor had come equipped with a rheostatically controlled red light, but quickly found that when the illumination was raised, the phenomena stopped altogether. Consequently, he turned the light down low.

After a considerable wait, the group was startled by a loud crash. When the main light was switched on, they found Chick (the sitter who was at that stage still thought of as the possible 'medium') lying on the floor. His chair had, he said, been pulled from under him 'as if by a steel hand'. Others too were to experience the unpleasant sensation of their chairs being moved from under them in total darkness, but Chick was the first to be completely toppled.

10
The Theory of the Medium

After this turbulent beginning, matters began to settle down a little. The sitters, growing accustomed to the oddities they were experiencing each week, grew calmer. Table movements — even violent table movements — were no longer quite so shocking as they had been. By the twenty-first meeting, the group was actually in a position where sitters could *request* the table to perform a specific action and the table would generally comply.

By about this time raps were beginning to occur, quite distinct from the earlier creakings. The occasional 'message' came through. During the twenty-third meeting, a regular group member, Miss P. M. Coghlan, found herself tilted along with the table when she sat on its top.

The substitution of a buzzer for the original lamp made little difference to the phenomena, nor did the introduction of additional sitters: on one occasion a total of eight witnessed levitations, movement without contact and another tilting of Miss Coghlan while seated on the table top. But a switch of the actual table and the introduction of cameras did seem to make a difference: there was an observable decline in the total number of raps and levitations — although Batcheldor remarks that these later recovered somewhat.

As the sequence of experiments continued, the 'energy' available to the group increased. Movements were definitely stronger — so strong, in fact, that three tables were actually smashed, including one with a tubular metal frame.

'Throughout the sequential development it became clear that a building process was going on,' wrote Batcheldor. 'New phenomena were being added, and once present tended to recur in subsequent meetings, though not necessarily with constant frequency.'

In his initial report, Batcheldor went on to examine the various phenomena in some detail. Among the more unusual was the 'gluing' effect. When this occurred, the table seemed stuck to the floor, sometimes all round, sometimes on one side but not the other. While gluing lasted, it was difficult (sometimes impossible) to move the table at all. But the effect tended to be short-lived and on at least one occasion was followed by a total levitation.

At the start of sessions, sitters often experienced curious breezes, mainly round the hands, as if they were being fanned. The sensation was too distinct to be confused with normal room draughts.

On a few occasions, the phenomenon of intense cold occurred. This was experienced under the table and to such an extent that the sitters pulled their legs away and winced. Curiously, holding a luminous plaque beneath the table intensified the cold.

The 'apports' mentioned earlier comprised a stone thrown across the room and a box of matches sprinkled about. There were also mysterious lights and the sensation of being touched, but Batcheldor, annoyingly, did not describe these in any detail since he considered observation of such phenomena unreliable.

Readers familiar with Spiritualist seances will by now have started to feel at home. Stripped of their religious overtones and underlying belief in post mortem communication, the similarities between seances and these early Batcheldor experiments are striking. This is particularly true of Victorian seances, where physical phenomena (apports, table turning, etc.) were much more commonplace than in modern Spiritualism.

Batcheldor himself obviously noted the similarities and although he was not concerned with talking to the dead, these similarities seem to have influenced his early train of thought.

The production of interesting phenomena is only one step. The next step is to try to explain how and why they occurred. The final step, for any worthwhile scientist, is to be able to repeat them to order.

Batcheldor had taken the first step successfully and to some extent was teetering on the third. But the explanations he was then considering were classical. He was looking for his medium.

Mediums are talented individuals capable of producing unusual effects. The term itself is Spiritualistic and unfortunate, since it suggests the individual is a channel, a sort of go-between for external forces or entities. Most Spiritualists, of course, would argue this is a precise description.

Historically, mediums have been thought capable of producing all the phenomena which occurred at the Batcheldor sittings; and more besides. In the Victorian heyday of 'physical mediumship', D. D. Home, who has already been mentioned in relation to levitation, seemed able to persuade accordions to play by themselves, small articles to materialize from thin air and live coals to burn on the palm of his hand without injury. At all times he believed himself to be in communication with spirits and considered it was the spirits who worked these feats, not himself.

Anyone embarking on any sort of investigation does so with certain fundamental premises: not all of them entirely conscious. Scientists are no exception. Early stalwarts of psychical research – Lodge, Myers, Sidgwick and the rest – assumed that in a typical seance, phenomena tended to originate from a single individual; and where the phenomena was considered genuine, it was that individual who became the focus of investigation.

Batcheldor initially made the same assumption. His friend W. G. Chick was cast in the role of the medium and considerable attention paid both to his *bona fides* and to influencing the phenomena through him.

'Since this paper was written,' states Batcheldor in a footnote, 'I have knelt beside W. G. C. [Chick] and held both his knees with one hand and both his thumbs with the other during a total levitation [of the table]. He remained quite still except for raising his hands with the table, and I am sure he did not grasp the table or use his legs. There was no evidence of the pin and ring trick or rod in sleeve, and no evidence that he is even acquainted with such methods.'

In an attempt to influence the phenomena, it was Chick who

was enclosed in a polythene bag up to his waist. (The table continued to tilt.)

There were, however, some occasions when the medium appeared not to be Chick but Miss Coghlan. This again is by no means unusual in Spiritualist seances. The theory is that seance room conditions are excellent for the development of mediumship so that spontaneous eruptions of the talent may occur among sitters who have not previously demonstrated psychism.

Had Batcheldor remained locked into the traditional notion of a medium, his experiments would have been interesting as a latter-day revival of a peculiar Victorian pastime. But they would not have been particularly useful to the average person who had neither personal psychical abilities nor very many lines of communication to proven mediums.

But Batcheldor did not remain locked in. As his experiments continued, he gradually moved away from the concept that the phenomena were caused by a medium and began to develop a different theory.

If accurate, it is a theory with profound consequences — and one which we shall examine in some detail presently.

11

The Search for Proof Positive

All this was going on in 1964. The first published reports did not appear until 1966. Meanwhile, Batcheldor began to establish other groups.

At first these ran in parallel with the original group on different days. Later they took over the main thrust of the investigation when the original group disbanded.

Two years after the publication of the Batcheldor Method in 1966, the first independent group began work at Grimsby under the leadership of D. W. Hunt. Soon this group too was producing effects up to and including table levitations.

In 1971, Colin Brookes-Smith, a close collaborator with Batcheldor in his experiments, organized an independent group of his own, following the Batcheldor approach but, as an engineer, concentrating more exclusively on the measurement of the phenomenon. Again, results were positive: so much so that Brookes-Smith was to write optimistically that, given suitable procedures, paranormal forces could be made available 'by the pound'.

Later still, a small group of professional people — a teacher, two psychologists and a social worker — began to use the Batcheldor method after failing to achieve results with Spiritualist techniques. Here too the method worked.

According to J. Isaacs, of the University of Aston in Birmingham, two further groups put Batcheldor's techniques to the test. One obtained spectacular levitations of a wicker chair, but despite the promising beginning, many members withdrew from the sittings shortly thereafter. The second of these groups, comprising university students, also abandoned their Batcheldor style experiments when they resulted in something resembling the start of a poltergeist outbreak.

By 1979, Batcheldor estimated that at least ten groups had achieved some degree of success with his methods independently of the original Exeter group. Over a fifteen-year period, this did not exactly represent a flood of interest, but it clearly demonstrated the Batcheldor approach was worth serious investigation. There was no doubt at all that something very peculiar occurred in groups adopting the Batcheldor techniques. The real problem was to validate its paranormal nature.

We will be examining Batcheldor's methodology in more detail at a later stage, but for the present it needs to be noted that the most successful sittings were held in total darkness. This is directly in line with Spiritualist experience; and Spiritualists have a theory to explain it. According to this theory, physical phenomena in the seance room can usually be explained by a substance called ectoplasm. Ectoplasm is believed to be a semi-physical substance somehow generated out of the medium's body. While ectoplasm is nebulous stuff, Spiritualists believe it can, under suitable circumstances, be sufficiently condensed to produce materializations and levitate objects. The problem is that it seems to be light-sensitive — hence the darkness of the typical seance room.

While Batcheldor had discovered, with the Spiritualists, that darkness tended to produce more spectacular phenomena, he did not accept the ectoplasm theory as the total answer. In this context, he pointed out that the dramatic levitations of poltergeist phenomena often occurred in broad daylight. The essential factor, he thought, was not light but sight.

This is a shrewd observation. Poltergeists are perhaps the most brutally physical of all paranormal phenomena, yet almost every case demonstrates one subtle yet maddeningly frustrating element. Even in the most violent poltergeist outbreak, it is difficult to find a witness who actually *saw* anything paranormal.

A glance through our earlier case studies demonstrates this point clearly. Windows are broken in *empty* rooms, so that no one actually sees it happen. Objects are found in peculiar places, but no one actually sees them being put there. Stones pound roofs or whiz past people's heads, but no one actually sees where they originate. John Bell may have been poisoned, and poison may have been in the medicine cupboard, but no one actually saw the liquid being poured down his sleeping throat.

In the course of his own experiments, Batcheldor notes that as the level of light increased, certain types of phenomena became increasingly difficult to obtain. But these were, in the main, phenomena which were witnessed primarily through the medium of *sight*. Raps (which by definition can never been seen, only heard) were comparatively easy to produce when the lighting level was high.

The question of sight observation and lighting levels made the problems of validation difficult. Even leaving aside direct visual observation, there are obviously a variety of other ways to demonstrate that the effects are genuine. Switchgear on the feet of the table is one obvious example; although while it can show a table has actually lifted, it cannot strictly rule out fraud.

But as Batcheldor tightened his scientific controls, he made another disturbing discovery. Every new control introduced had the observable effect of reducing the phenomena. Once the controls became watertight, the phenomena stopped altogether.

Batcheldor suspected he knew the reason and in an attempt to get around it tried introducing new controls gradually. This approach seemed to work, up to a point, in that the level of phenomena would initially fall, then slowly rise again as the group became accustomed to working within the confines of the latest control. But once the final loophole was plugged, the phenomena would almost invariably stop.

A process of delayed validation was also attempted. That is to say, circumstances were arranged so that no one could say whether or not a particular phenomenon was paranormal at the time it occurred. The final verdict would be delivered (by instrumental means) at a later time.

This method did not work very well either. The group found that either nothing happened in these circumstances; or that phenomena did indeed occur, but the recording apparatus developed a mysterious fault at the critical moment.

None of this is particularly new. I must be among several hundred (perhaps several thousand) psychical investigators to have experienced the persistent breakdown of mechanical devices during a particularly interesting experiment. On one occasion, while attempting to record some highly evidential trance material, I managed to destroy a perfectly good cassette recorder. The engineer who tried to repair it remarked that the insides were 'the weirdest mess' he had ever seen. Lyall Watson reported the same sort of thing happening when scientists attempted to film 'pyschic surgery' operations in the Phillipines. Motors jammed, lights failed. The results of one operation — a gallstone being taken back to the States for study — vanished from a hermetically sealed jar during the plane trip.

Coupled with the fact that mediums perform less and less effectively under increasingly stringent test conditions, this sort of thing has long convinced a majority of scientists that supposedly paranormal effects are misinterpretations at best and outright fraud at worst.

It is a tempting conclusion, but one which Batcheldor never came to share. Commonsense factors like trust in his colleagues and his own powers of observation had convinced him that the effects his techniques produced were indeed paranormal. Experience and familiarity with the history of psychical research suggested that attempts at absolute validation (in the scientific sense) might well prove a waste of time. Rather than attempting to go over the same vain ground, he developed two working hypotheses:

1. that at least some of the effects were indeed paranormal;
2. that some factor inherent in their production resisted strict validation.

He then set about trying to discover the hidden factor in the second hypothesis. This led to the formation of a third theory: that the act of *observation* might directly influence paranormal events.

This theory is not quite so outlandish as it sounds. Something similar has long been adopted in the realm of sub-nuclear physics where scientists have recognized that attempts to measure one aspect of particle behaviour completely preclude the possibility of measuring other aspects: a different way of saying that the act of observation must be considered an integral part of the phenomenon itself.

It is difficult idea for the layperson to grasp. It is even quite a difficult notion for the scientists and in physics only the introduction of mathematical models of particle behaviour made it tenable at all. Batcheldor is a psychologist, not a mathematician, and his approach to the problem involved a psychological model.

He came to consider that the reason why tighter controls dampened down phenomena was that the use of controls adversely influenced the minds of the sitters. And since it was the minds of the sitters which produced the phenomena in the first place, their collective attitude was vital for positive results.

In the course of his experiments, Batcheldor came to consider that controls mitigated against phenomena in three ways.

First, they tended to introduce an element of doubt. The group mindset changed from 'it will work as usual' to 'Will it work in these new circumstances?' In other words, belief began to waver. He called this phenomenon 'intellectual resistance'.

The second problem was that controls tended to increase fear among the participants. If the experiment were to succeed under rigidly controlled conditions, it would no longer be possible to explain away the paranormal.

'When we *really* encounter the paranormal, it is at first rather frightening,' he wrote to me during the preparation of this book. 'While fear itself will not stop the phenomena because fear implies intense belief and belief stimulates positive results, a lot depends on how we handle the fear. If we become mentally paralysed by it, the phenomena may well escalate in an uncontrollable way, as happened with Isaac's students. But if we fight against the fear, by telling ourselves that nothing is going to happen, we may ruin the experiment and prevent the attempted validation from succeeding. Very often this takes place more or less unconsciously — a process I call "emotional resistance".

The third problem arises from the fact that tight controls exclude what Batcheldor calls 'artifacts' — somethng we shall be examining in more detail a little later. At this stage it is enough to say that Batcheldor believes artifacts to be of the utmost importance in starting the whole PK process going, since they help produce a mindset of intense belief.

It will readily be seen from this that Batcheldor had, by now, abandoned his early ideas that a single medium was at work. A broadening of his experience with various groups convinced him no special 'psychic' talent was needed. The effects were produced by the group itself, not by any particular individual or individuals within it.

To some extent, he was able to validate his mindset theory. The crucial test is perhaps best given in his own words:

> It occurred to me that a deliberate attempt could be made to inhibit the interfering thoughts that arise at the crucial moment of a test or when making a clear observation of paranormality.

> On one occasion we were obtaining levitations of a cardboard tube (like a Spiritualist 'trumpet') with top finger contact, and I had a camera and flash ready to which I had drawn no special attention.

> When the tube levitated, I picked up the camera with my free (right) hand and, without warning the other sitters in the total darkness, took a photograph.

> I have practised 'blanking' my mind and did so as best I could while taking the photograph (I think I even thought the experiment would not work, and did not care much either way). The result was the best, and practically the only, photograph of a levitation we ever obtained. It showed all fingers pretty clearly on top and the tube about a foot above the floor.

> It should be noted that the other sitters did not need to blank

their minds because they were not expecting the photograph to be taken. Subsequent sight of the photograph was mildly shocking to the group and there were signs of reluctance to repeat the experience and of a wish to explain the presence of the photograph away (e.g. by assuming that the fingers are somehow gripping the tube).

Relevant to this theme is the fact that when sitters trained themselves to inhibit discursive thinking, the levitated table or tube remained suspended in the air for a much longer period, whereas any intrusive thought caused it to come crashing down.

The theory of sitters' mental attitude, developed out of the difficulties experienced in validating phenomena, not only began to explain why direct validation had proven virtually impossible in the past, but also went a long way towards refining the Batcheldor Method so that it could be successfully applied by any group who cared to try it.

12

The Witchdoctor Syndrome

Folk wisdom maintains that faith can move mountains. Whether or not this is true, it can certainly move milers.

The phenomenon of the first four-minute mile, now part of athletic history, has long fascinated me. When I was a boy, the consensus of sporting — and, indeed, medical — opinion held that a four-minute mile was a physical impossibility. This pessimistic theory was based on the premise that the human body must have ultimate limitations and the observable fact that milers of the day, while sometimes approaching the magical four-minute figure, never managed to pass it.

Obviously not everyone believed a four-minute mile was impossible. Runners continued to try for it, trainers continued to attempt new and different approaches. Nothing worked. Until, that is, the day Dr Roger Bannister ran the first sub-four-minute mile.

Bannister was a fit, thoroughly trained athlete. Nonetheless, he was on the point of collapse when he had passed the tape. Watching the event, one might have been excused for concluding that the run was a freak, the once-in-a-lifetime effort of a superman. In point of fact, it proved to be nothing of the sort. Within weeks of Bannister's record-shattering performance, a sub-four-minute mile had been run again by another athlete. Within a year, such runs had become commonplace.

All this is a matter of record and it raises one extremely interesting question. If no one on earth could run a mile in less than four minutes during the year *before* Bannister broke the record, why could so many different athletes manage the feat during the year *after?*

It has to be noted that Bannister introduced no dramatic new running techniques or training methods. He discovered no particular trick. He simply trained as athletes had always trained, and ran as athletes had always run.

Yet, manifestly, there was a Before and After difference. But to find it, you have to look beyond the purely physical aspects of competitive sport. How Bannister managed a four-minute mile is a matter of possible conjecture. How those who followed him managed a four-minute mile is not: they made their achievement *because somebody had proven conclusively it could be done.*

What we are talking about here is mindset. At one point of time, the collective mindset of the athletic community considered a four-minute mile a physical impossibility. When Bannister breasted the tape, he shattered that mindset along with the world record. From a conviction that the feat was physically impossible, the athletic community moved overnight to a position of knowledge that it was possible after all. This mental shift did not, of course, turn every runner into a four-minute-miler. But it was more than enough to take the psychological brakes off the runners who already had the physical capacity for such a feat.

It is a commonplace observation that mental attitude (mindset) has enormous influence on human achievement in all sorts of diverse activities. So long as illness is believed to be the Will of God, medicine makes few strides. So long as the earth is believed to be the centre of the universe, astronomy stagnates. So long as a business considers its markets saturated, sales figures continue to decline.

Mindset works against achievement in two ways, one obvious, one far more subtle.

The obvious way is that it prevents attempts being made in the first place. If you are persuaded that the world is flat, you will hardly waste your time trying to sail round it.

The more subtle way is that it acts — often quite mysteriously — against success in the venture which is experimentally attempted. This is a point worth fuller discussion since it is central to the application and understanding of the Batcheldor Method.

While Batcheldor's approach involves analysis of the negative factors, we may begin by examining the mechanism of belief in general.

At one stage of my career I worked with a clinical psychologist who used hypnosis in the treatment of tension, smoking and weight problems. Part of his own rather chequered background was a period as a stage hypnotist. In his clinical practice, he quickly discovered that those patients who were aware of his reputation as an entertainer responded far better to hypnotic induction than those who were not. The experience led him to coin his theory of the Witchdoctor Syndrome.

As its name implies, the Witchdoctor Syndrome is especially prevalent in primitive societies. Through cultural conditioning (often reinforced by initiation rites at puberty which have the effect of weeding out the less suggestible members) the tribe is fundamentally convinced of the 'magical' powers of its witchdoctors. And this conviction goes a long way towards making the powers a reality.

There is a dramatic example of the process in action among the Aborigines of Australia. Part of Aborigine custom embodies the myth of the 'pointing bone'. It is believed that by using a small, specially prepared sliver of bone, a witchdoctor has merely to point to cause death.

White settlers quickly discovered that pointing bones worked. The unfortunate tribesman on the receiving end would sicken, weaken and die over a period varying from a few days to a few weeks. Nor could all the advances of Western medicine discover the cause of the mysterious malady, let alone cure it.

But if pointing bones worked, they worked only on Aborigines. Whites seemed to be naturally immune. Since essentially the same process had been observed in relation to African and other 'magical' practices, psychologists quickly concluded that the essence of the magic lay not in the witchdoctor, but in the victim. It was the victim's *belief* in the curse which eventually killed him.

This is well in line with current psychosomatic theory. There is no longer the slightest doubt that the human mind can influence the human body in all sorts of ways — many of them extremely destructive, as any tense and ulcerated executive will quickly attest. Thus the mind of the Aborigine victim, convinced of the power of the pointing bone, instructed his body to sicken and die. The body inevitably responded.

My psychologist colleague took the theory of the Witchdoctor Syndrome out of its primitive tribal context and extended it into our own more sophisticated culture. We no longer believe in witchdoctors, but we remain quite willing to be convinced that certain individuals — and indeed classes of individuals — have abilities beyond the average. In certain circumstances, this very belief enables the individuals in question to function more effectively. Stage hypnosis is a case in point. As the entertainer builds a reputation, audience expectation of his abilities increases. This produces a sort of positive feedback. As more members of the audience become convinced the entertainer can hypnotize them, they drop their barriers and permit themselves to be hypnotized. This, in turn, reinforces the belief pattern of the remainder.

Essentially the same thing occurs in medicine. A good reputation can provide a general practitioner with as valuable a healing tool as a good bedside manner. As the Aborigine's mind instructed his body to die, so the patient's mind instructs his body to get better.

The process is even more striking in certain areas of fringe medicine: notably faith healing carried out in a religious context. Anyone who has attended 'divine healing' services will usually be struck (and sometimes alarmed) by the degree to which stage management is used to instil and reinforce certain belief patterns in the congregation. William Sargant, in an examination of mind control, noted the striking similarities between brainwashing techniques and the practices of certain religious sects. But it is not the techniques which are at issue here: merely the end result. In many a divine healing service, belief among the congregation rises to peaks of hysteria.

So far, very few psychologists would disagree radically with anything that has been claimed for the Witchdoctor Syndrome. But then again, we have only examined one aspect of the

Syndrome itself. There is a second side to the coin; and one which is, admittedly, a little more controversial.

Colonel H. S. Olcott, the Victorian gentleman who, with Madame H. P. Blavatsky, founded the Theosophical Society, records a curious experience which occurred during one of his trips to India.

For reasons not entirely clear, one of Olcott's native servants became convinced the Colonel was a powerful magician with great healing abilities. The fancy persuaded him to bring a sick friend to Olcott for cure. The problem was that Olcott had no healing talents whatsoever. He did, however, have a kind heart and a knowledge of psychology. Unwilling to turn away the sick native, Olcott decided to play on his own reputation. If the native believed that Olcott was a powerful magician, then it was reasonable to suppose that the force of his belief, properly directed, might help rid his body of illness. In effect, Olcott applied the Witchdoctor Syndrome. Rising to his full height and adopting his sternest Victorian mien, he pointed towards the patient and intoned solemnly: 'Be cured!'

The Witchdoctor Syndrome did its work. The native felt an upsurge of wellbeing, pronounced himself better and ran off to tell his friends. As a result, Olcott was soon plagued with a front hall full of sick and dying Indians, all hoping for another miracle. Unable to do anything else, Olcott did the best he could.

And at this point, the second aspect of the Witchdoctor Syndrome suddenly emerged. Olcott's original self-image of a retired soldier was gradually replaced by a self-image of a healer. Intellectually he knew, of course, that his patients were healing themselves: yet a number of the cures were so dramatic that Olcott began to wonder if he might actually have hitherto unsuspected healing powers.

No sooner had this suspicion taken firm root than genuine healing powers began to emerge. Olcott became aware of subtle energy flows within his own body. Like Dr Rhine's psychokinetic gambler, he found there were times when he felt 'hot' — a subjective conviction that he could work healing miracles. At such times he consistently produced results which could not, he thought, be explained purely in terms of the patient's belief.

Like the barrier of the four-minute mile, this story — and several similar — interests me greatly. While the likelihood of my ever running a four-minute (or even an eight-minute) mile is remote, I have had personal experience of the reverse Witchdoctor Syndrome which turned Olcott from a psychologist playing at healing to a genuine healer.

This experience arose out of a study of alternative healing techniques — notably acupuncture, hypnotherapy and reflexology. While I had no medical ambitions whatsoever, emergency situations occasionally arose in which I was forced to apply some of the theoretical techniques. That they frequently worked was more luck than good judgement and the results were, of course, applicable purely to the automatic action of the techniques themselves.

But this was only how I saw the situation. Within a small circle of friends and acquaintances I began, over the years, to acquire an inadvertent — and most unwelcome — reputation as a healer. This was perhaps inevitable in retrospect. To the average person, acupuncture, hypnosis and the rest are often seen as 'magical' techniques, a belief enhanced by their rarity value.

How one is seen by others has, of course, a profound influence on how one sees oneself. At a conscious level, I never came to see myself as anything more than a dabbler in emergency techniques. But the positive feedback I received over the years obviously unlocked something previously well buried in my mind, for the day came when, like Olcott, I 'got hot' and experienced an utter conviction that I would produce positive results in a particular medical problem. This conviction has recurred at intervals since then and each time has fully justified itself in terms of treatment. If it is an illusion, it is a particularly compelling illusion which, so long as results remain positive, is self-sustaining and self-reinforcing.

13

A Question of Conviction

All of us confuse beliefs with facts. This is particularly easy to see in the historical context. There was a time when everyone knew the earth was flat. It was self-evident. There was a time when everyone knew the sun went round the earth. That too was self-evident: you only had to look up to see the proof.

Things like this were not thought of as beliefs. They were thought of as facts — which is another way of saying they were not generally thought of at all, only taken for granted.

There are a whole host of beliefs which have fallen into this category, sometimes throughout the broad spread of population, sometimes confined to select groups. All share the same common denominator: they are, so long as they endure, unquestioned assumptions.

The unquestioned assumptions of other ages are usually easy to spot — especially if they have subsequently been proven wrong. It is far less easy to recognize that our own age and culture is just as much a prey to these psychological dynamics as any in the past.

In this context, it is interesting to contrast the twentieth century with the twelfth. In the twelfth century, any systematic investigation into natural law was held to be heretical and dangerous. In the twentieth, such investigation is held to be the only road to progress. In the twelfth century, miracles were only rare. In the twentieth, they are actually impossible.

Assumptions about what is possible or impossible are perhaps the determining factor in the forward thrust of any culture. While you remain convinced the earth is flat, you are effectively precluded from any thought of sailing round it. At the individual level, these same assumptions act as a barrier against personal achievement.

But at the individual level, the situation is complicated by additional factors. A conviction that something is impossible may stop you ever attempting to achieve it. But should you be persuaded (against your better judgement) to make the attempt, your fundamental conviction will almost certainly act to block success.

In one of my earlier books, I gave a straightforward illustration of this point. If you were to take a plank, two feet wide and fifteen feet long, and lay it on the ground, almost anyone could walk along its length without the slightest difficulty. But the same plank, placed over a bottomless crevass, becomes an immediate impossibility. The dimensions of the plank have not changed. What has changed — dramatically — is the individual perception of success. More to the point, the average individual forced to walk such a plank would almost certainly fall off. His conviction that the feat is impossible acts to make it so.

All of us reach adult life well equipped with a whole collection of convictions about what is possible and what is not. And because we confuse beliefs with facts, such convictions are very seldom examined, let alone questioned. But beliefs, however firmly held, are *not* facts — or at best not necessarily facts.

What we are examining here is the collision between common sense and experience on the one hand, and actuality on the other. Common sense and experience both tell you that your mind is your own, and that telepathy is impossible. Rhine's experiments have shown this to be untrue. Common sense and experience both tell you that the walls of your house are solid. Physicists have demonstrated that they actually comprise mainly empty space, with their overall form no more than a statistical probability.

Such demonstrations make very little difference to the way we behave. We are slow learners and attitudes of mind persist long after the evidence has made them obsolete. This is particularly true in the realms of psychical research. As we have already seen, a great many scientists have worked hard over a great many years to demonstrate the actuality of things like telepathy, clairvoyance, precognition and PK. For most of us, this has not made the slightest difference to the way we live or think. We do not, for instance, attempt to develop personal powers of telepathy, however substantial a saving it would make on our phone bills. We do not tackle the fuel crisis by calling up our own PK abilities.

It might be argued that many people have the excuse of ignorance. The findings of parapsychologists have never been the subject of page one headlines in the morning paper and, surprising though it may seem to those interested in the subject, the average person has never even heard of Dr Rhine. But even those who have carefully studied the evidence and accepted the findings do not, by and large, behave any differently to the norm. There has been no discernible outbreak of wild talents within the scientific community engaged in the study of psychical phenomena.

There is little doubt that if you are to develop any personal talent, you must accept a series of premises. First, you must accept that the talent itself actually exists. Secondly, you must accept that it can be developed. Thirdly, you must accept that it can be developed *in you*.

But it seems that intellectual acceptance is not enough. It is no good recognizing that in theory you might become a telepath because telepathy has been shown to be a statistical reality. What is needed is an *emotional* conviction, a certainty so deeply rooted that it shatters all your previously held beliefs on the subject.

Most of our fundamental belief patterns are not a matter of experience, but of cultural conditioning. This comes about partly through parental training, partly, and much more subtly, by the general attitudes of the society in which we happen to find ourselves. A study of history makes this latter point clear. It is uncommonly difficult for an individual to sustain a belief that differs radically from generally accepted ideas — to remain convinced that the world is round in a society where everyone knows perfectly well it is flat.

The question of conviction has been well examined in the field of business — particularly in relation to sales techniques. It is commonly accepted that a salesperson's ability to move a product is directly related to his faith in the product's performance.

To some extent, this is easily explained. Faith in the product gives the salesperson confidence and lends conviction to the selling message. But there is a further factor. Conviction is contagious. The psychological mechanics of the transfer of faith are not readily apparent, but the phenomenon is observable in many selling transactions.

In the United States particularly, the dynamics of selling are well understood, and considerable time, effort and money are expended on sales training. This training will commonly include a full and detailed grounding in the product itself, with emphasis on generating a high degree of enthusiasm in the sales staff.

These observations may seem a long way from our examination of PK, but they are not. The success of such sales training methods suggests that particular belief patterns can be instilled or reinforced. They can also be changed: a trick which happens frequently when a salesperson moves to a competing company.

By taking sales training as our example, rather than the more obvious, complex and emotionally charged examples of brain-washing or religious conversion, it is possible to observe some of the factors which create belief. Perhaps the most important is the 'show me' factor.

It has been recognized for generations that the most potent selling technique is demonstration. Car advertising invariably includes an invitation to test-drive. A multitude of differing products are offered on the basis of a free trial. Potential purchasers are continually urged to see for themselves, because seeing, it seems, really is believing.

But the 'show me' factor operates far beyond the world of business. How often have you remarked cynically that you 'will believe it when you see it'? And how often has the evidence of your own observation carried far greater weight than a mass of second-hand evidence?

It is perfectly possible to develop intellectual convictions by studying written documentation, but emotional conviction generally only follows a convincing demonstration.

This is, of course, what happened with the four-minute mile. Dr Bannister gave a convincing demonstration (filmed and widely distributed) that the feat was possible. In the same context, but closer to our subject matter, Batcheldor reports briefly on a group which successfully mounted a Philip-type experiment *after watching a film of the original*.

Substantially the same situation arose when the Israeli psychic Uri Geller demonstrated fork-bending on television: almost immediately there were reports of viewers duplicating the feat up and down the country. (Perhaps significantly, a great many of these viewers were schoolchildren, whose preconceptions about what is and is not possible are less firmly set than those of adults.)

It is interesting to note the demonstration does not have to be genuine. All that is required is that we *believe* it to be genuine. This is the principle which underlies Batcheldor's use of 'artifacts' in the process by which gross PK phenomena are generated.

Since this is considered by Batcheldor to be of supreme importance to his system — and also seen by some observers to be his most important contribution to psychical research — it may be as well to introduce the artifact concept in his own words.

Artifacts enable perfectly ordinary people with undisciplined minds to achieve moments of complete faith (or conviction) without any effort at all, and without any mental training.

Artifacts are normal events mistaken for paranormal events. They therefore produce a moment of intense belief that success has already been achieved. This intense belief then produces a genuine phenomenon. This in turn stimulates more belief, and so the process carries on.

Artifacts are of two kinds, deliberate, and accidental or spontaneous.

The deliberate kind are equivalent to cheating, so cheating is psi-conducive (a fact that has been known and exploited by witchdoctors for a long time).

However, contrary to a widespread misconception, I do *not* recommend the use of cheating in a B-group, since it leads to confusion. Development can, and should, take place entirely on the basis of accidental or spontaneous artifacts. Provided tight controls are not imposed, there are always plenty of these, such as accidental sights, sounds, and movements, especially in the dark.

But the most important spontaneous artifacts are movements of the table due to unconscious muscular action or UMA. These provide an excellent illusion that the table is being moved by a mysterious independent force.

Provided there is not too much initial scepticism this creates intense belief which in turn generates real PK — leading to stronger and more varied movements and eventually to levitations and movements without contact.

Similarly, accidental creaks lead to genuinely paranormal raps; accidental visual phenomena lead to psychic lights; etc., etc.

The artifact-induction principle is applied in many areas of psychic phenomena besides seances and sitter-groups: e.g., in poltergeists and paranormal healing. 'Illusory success' is frequently the main thing which breaks through our habitual or conditioned modes of thinking in which 'the paranormal cannot happen'.

Alongside demonstration as a belief generator comes the acceptance of the belief by a peer group. Testimonial advertising works on this principle, as do claims of high volume sales. If the group believes, the individual tends to believe as well. More importantly, in certain circumstances, the individual actually needs the support of the group to sustain his or her own belief.

Group support is particularly important in the realm of unusual phenomena, even where demonstration has managed to instil an initial conviction. Paranormal occurrences are uncomfortable to live with. We have already mentioned Isaacs' report of the student group which abandoned a Batcheldor-style experiment because they became frightened. But even where fear is not a direct factor, experience of the paranormal runs so contrary to our established belief patterns that there is a very widespread — and very human — tendency to shy away from the evidence.

In my own experience as an investigator, I have noticed how often and how quickly a great many people actually manage to *forget* the unusual in their own lives. A reported case might be categorically denied as ever having happened within a year of the occurrence — possibly indicative of emotional resistance. Closely allied to this tendency is the desire to find a 'normal' explanation — almost at any cost. Individuals who would feel insulted if you questioned their mental competence in any other situation are quite prepared to suggest they hallucinated when they saw a ghost. Batcheldor again noted this phenomenon when he took his evidential photograph of the trumpet levitation. Once the print was shown around, a great deal of energy was expended in an attempt to demonstrate the picture did not actually show what it seemed to show.

In a solitary experience of the paranormal, old belief patterns come into direct conflict with the demonstration and sometimes win. In such cases, the commonplace 'Seeing is believing' is replaced by the almost as commonplace 'I saw it, but I don't believe it.' And even where the experience is accepted as genuine, there remains the danger that it will quickly be forgotten as the original belief patterns gradually re-establish themselves despite the evidence.

When, however, a paranormal experience is shared with others, these tendencies are not nearly so marked. Doubts about one's powers of observation (or even sanity!) cannot be so readily sustained if others saw the same thing. And group amnesia seldom occurs after the event.

In the remainder of this book, we shall be closely examining the means by which you — a normal, non-mediumistic, non-psychic reader — can produce gross PK effects. The techniques used are those developed by Batcheldor, whose work in the field over the past decades has enabled the phenomena to be generated repeatedly by virtually anyone with the will and patience to put the methods into practice.

In the course of his own experiments, Batcheldor came to accept that the crucial factor in success was the very one we have been examining – the belief patterns of the participants. In our present culture, the dominant mindset strongly suggests PK is quite impossible. Whatever reports might emanate from Russia, common sense and experience tell us all that objects simply do not move of their own accord – and if they seem to, then there must be some natural explanation.

This mindset is a fact which must be faced – and overcome – if results are to be achieved. Much of the Batcheldor methodology – which we shall return to shortly – is geared towards that single fact.

14

Improving your Mindreach

Although this book has so far concentrated almost exclusively on PK in its various manifestations, experience shows there is no clear dividing line between differing psychical abilities – no clear dividing line, that is, which has not been self-imposed.

This point was very clearly illustrated when I was running a series of computerized ESP tests on an Irish psychic. Two programs were being used in the experiments. The first was a straightforward adaptation of Rhine's Zener card techniques. The program, which tested for precognition, required the subject to guess which symbol would be next shown on the computer screen. The symbol was then shown and the subject invited to continue. After a run of guesses, the computer would calculate the number of accurate predictions and evaluate the probabilities of the precognitive factor.

Since the symbols shown by the computer were randomly selected, the final readout gave a highly accurate evaluation of psi potential, provided there was a sufficiently long run of guesses to work on.

The second program used exactly the same technical procedure, but in a very different form.

In this test, the subject was presented with a graphic representation of five boxes on screen and told that one of them contained $1 million. The subject was then required to guess which box had the money.

Once the guess was made, the computer would 'open the box', indicating whether or not it was empty. The subject's monetary score (if any) was then displayed. Here again, over a run of guesses, the program was designed to use probability calculus in order to determine the chance odds against a particular score — and hence the odds in favour of a psi element in the subject's guesses.

Like the first program, the computer played the money game by randomly selecting a box for the $1 million *after* the guess was made. This meant, of course, that any psi significant score must demonstrate precognitive potential, exactly as in the first program.

Interestingly, my Irish subject (who was familiar with Rhine's Zener techniques) consistently produced significant scores when tested by the first program. In several instances, the probability of precognition ran into odds of many thousands to one.

But this same subject was equally consistent in failing to show any psi talent whatsoever when tested by the second program. There was little mystery as to the reason. Although she clearly recognized her psychical abilities, she was fundamentally convinced she was 'unlucky' in financial matters.

Since the essential structure of the two programs was identical, it became obvious that the single factor which varied between the two sets of tests was the subject's level of self-confidence. She *believed* she could correctly predict the run of Zener cards. She *believed* she could not possibly locate $1 million — even in a game situation.

In other words, her belief had effectively limited the manifestation of an ability that was undoubtedly and demonstrably there.

This is the same point that Batcheldor has made repeatedly in relation to gross PK phenomena in a group context. The central problem is always that of convincing members of the group that the exercise is possible in the first place. Once that problem is solved, it is a relatively short step to creating a conviction that the exercise is possible *for the group*.

Several years ago, an imaginative researcher with a talent for coining phrases, decided to investigate the point statistically by dividing test subjects into two categories — 'Sheep', who believed implicitly in psychical abilities, and 'Goats', who considered the notion of such abilities to be nonsense.

Both groups, when scientifically tested, produced their quota of high-scoring subjects, but with one very important difference. The Sheep showed high *positive* ESP scores. The Goats showed high *negative* scores. (A word of explanation may not go amiss here. In a well designed Zener card experiment, *any* large deviation from chance expectation must be considered significant. This is fairly obvious when a subject scores well above chance expectation. But a score that is well below chance expectation must be considered significant too. Thus, while the Sheep used their psychical talents to support their own conviction that ESP was a reality, the Goats used theirs in order ironically to prove that ESP was nonsense.)

It is probably fair to speculate that the majority of readers of a book of this type are more likely to be Sheep than Goats. Nonetheless, even Sheep find difficulty in moving from a belief in the reality of psychical phenomena to a belief that they themselves are able to produce it.

For this reason, the first step in extending your mindreach must be to demonstrate (to your own satisfaction at least) that you have some psi talent. To do so, you will require a reliable means of testing such talent and some indication of the methods which may be used to bring it from a latent to an active state.

There are a number of ways in which psychical ability may be demonstrated. A biographer of Aleister Crowley, an occultist who developed a sinister reputation in his lifetime, has described one method by which Crowley showed his own peculiar abilities.

The demonstration took place in a Paris street. Crowley invited his companion to select a passer-by at random. This was duly done and the intended 'victim' pointed out — a middle-aged man with a walking stick, obviously out for a brisk afternoon stroll.

Crowley moved off and began to walk behind the man, drawing closer and closer without, however, attracting his attention. After a few moments, Crowley was so close to the Parisian that only a few inches separated them. At this point, Crowley began to synchronize his movements with that of the man, so that to an observer they appeared like two children engaged in the comical game of 'Ducks'.

Crowley's companion noted that not only did Crowley synchronize his leg and arm movements with those of the walker, but also synchronized his breathing. After a few minutes of this curious business, Crowley abruptly and deliberately collapsed on the pavement. At once, the walker collapsed too.

Neither was hurt, although the middle-aged Parisian was totally bewildered as to why he should suddenly have fallen as he did. In fact, there is no ready explanation outside the curious world of psi phenomena. Within that context, however, it is easy to postulate that Crowley simply formed a psychical link with the walker and used it to influence his actions.

One would not, of course, recommend Crowley's childish games to any serious reader. But it is true to suggest that perhaps the simplest test of psi ability may be carried out in much the same sort of situation: in a street, a bus, a cinema, theatre or some similar public place.

Place yourself *behind* your intended subject and stare fixedly, with concentration at the nape of his neck. There is a strong likelihood that, within a few minutes of your beginning this little experiment, he will grow uneasy and eventually turn around.

This technique is by no means novel. It is, in fact, so well known that you may actually have used it at some time as an amusement. But its very familiarity tends to blind us to how difficult the results of this experiment are to explain. Why *should* someone grow uneasy and turn simply because you happen to be staring at them? What influence reaches out to produce the observable result? Neither common sense nor science has a ready answer, leaving us with the virtual certainty that the reason must lie in the psychical realm.

If you care to attempt this experiment a few times with different subjects and find that you achieve consistently positive results, then you may reasonably conclude that, whatever your preconceptions, you have some form of operative psi talent. Precisely what this amounts to is another question, but one which need not detain us here. All we are doing is examining some methods by which you may convince yourself you can do something generally considered impossible. And despite the naïve simplicity of this initial test, the fact remains that influencing someone without speech or contact *is* generally considered impossible. Yet if your subject turns, this is exactly what you have done.

If you happen to have hypnotic abilities — and a great many people do — you might care to structure a much more sophisticated example of the same experiment. A vast body of Russian research, as well as some early work done in Britain, suggests it is perfectly possible to place a subject in trance telepathically: and even to persuade him to carry out telepathic commands. There is no great trick to setting up such an experiment, provided you accept two caveats. The first is that your subject should be readily hypnotizable — preferably someone you have worked with before. The second is that the subject should not be told the nature of the experiment in advance. To do so will negate any apparent results since most subjects are perfectly capable of falling into trance spontaneously as a result of an *implied* suggestion.

But whatever you feel about street games, it is clear that anyone who has a serious intent to improve their mindreach must require a more reliable method of self-testing — preferably one that not only indicates the presence of psi talent, but also the *level* at which it manifests.

Such a test will initially enable you to determine whether your natural psi abilities are at all operational and will subsequently show you to what degree practice may have developed them.

Fortunately such a test is readily available, based on the work of Rhine that we have already mentioned.

15

Computer Psi Test

The proliferation of home computer systems has created a situation where a great many interested individuals may accurately test themselves and their friends for psi potential with no more difficulty than it takes to set up and run a program.

Not all psi elements are particularly suited to computerized testing. Telepathy, for example, is by definition a mind-to-mind contact, and while computers frequently behave as if they have minds of their own, the consensus of reasonable opinion remains that they do not. Thus telepathic talent is best tested between two (or more) humans with the computer playing its part only in calculating the odds.

Precognition and clairvoyance (the ability to sense events at a distance) are, by contrast, ideally suited to computer testing, since the possibility of human error is rendered virtually non-existent.

While what follows will, in general, lie within these latter two areas, it is not suggested that the tests be considered specific. We are seeking only to determine your level (if any) of psi talent; and if such talent manifests, it should not matter at this stage precisely what category it falls into.

Those of you who do not own, or have access to, a computer system should skip the remainder of this chapter and go on to the next, where essentially the same ground is covered in a different way. The same holds good for those whose systems do not operate in BASIC, unless you happen to have the technical skill to translate a BASIC listing into the language of your own computer.

For those who remain with us, the following listing is of a program which will enable your computer to evaluate your psychical potential fairly quickly and accurately, and will allow you, in turn, to monitor any changes in your abilities that may subsequently arise.

The program itself is written in Applesoft and will run, without change, on any Apple computer having that language available and sufficient memory capacity. For those using a different dialect of BASIC the program has been carefully annotated so that the necessary conversion changes may be easily made.

To make the program operational, you should carefully type it into your system, SAVE it to disc or tape for future use, then RUN it in order to take your first test.

If you find the program is not RUNning as it should, then check that you have typed it in accurately. Here again, the appended notes will be useful in helping you find the particular program segment where the trouble lies.

ESP TEST PROGRAM LISTING

(All REM lines may be omitted)

```
10 REM INITIALIZE VARIABLES
20 TR = 0:AC = 0:N = 0:G = 0:PR = 0:OC = 0
30 REM ERROR TRAPPING
40 ONERR GOTO 750
50 REM SET UP TITLE
60 HOME : VTAB 12: HTAB 14: PRINT "E.S.P. TEST": HTAB 14:
PRINT "***********": FOR J = 1 TO 2000: NEXT :TR = 0
70 REM INSTRUCTIONS OPTION
80 HOME : VTAB 12: HTAB 10: PRINT "INSTRUCTIONS (Y/N)?":::
GET A$: IF A$ < > "Y" AND A$ < > "N" THEN 80
90 IF A$ = "Y" THEN GOSUB 580
100 REM SET NUMBER OF RUNS TO VARIABLE "N"
110 HOME : INVERSE : PRINT "YOU MAKE 25 GUESSES PER
RUN": NORMAL : VTAB 12: PRINT "HOW MANY RUNS OF THE
CARDS IN THIS TEST?": PRINT : GET N: IF N < 1 THEN 110
```

120 HOME: VTAB 10: HTAB 5: PRINT "PLEASE TAKE A MOMENT TO RELAX.": PRINT : HTAB 4: PRINT "HIT ANY KEY WHEN READY TO BEGIN": PRINT : GET A$

130 REM OUTER LOOP SETS NUMBER OF RUNS

140 REM INNER LOOP SETS 25 CARDS PER RUN

150 FOR J = 1 TO N: FOR C = 1 TO 25: GOSUB 290: NEXT : NEXT

160 REM ANNOUNCE RESULT CALCULATION

170 HOME : VTAB 12: INVERSE : PRINT "COMPUTING RESULT . . . . PLEASE WAIT": NORMAL : FOR J = 1 TO 2000: NEXT

180 REM CALCULATE PERCENTAGE OF CORRECT GUESSES

190 HOME :P = (TR / (N * 25)) * 100

200 PRINT "YOU MADE"; TR;" CORRECT GUESSES.": PRINT : PRINT "THIS REPRESENTS "; P;"% ACCURACY."

210 REM ANNOUNCE PSI SCORE IF ANY

220 IF PR > 120 THEN VTAB 12: HTAB 15: FLASH : PRINT "PSI SCORE": NORMAL : PRINT : PRINT "YOUR ESP RATING CURRENTLY STANDS AT "; PR: PRINT : PRINT "THIS MEANS THE ODDS AGAINST YOUR SCORE": PRINT : PRINT "BEING DUE TO CHANGE ARE "; PR;" TO ONE!": GOTO 260

230 VTAB 12: PRINT "YOUR ESP RATING CURRENTLY STANDS AT " ;PR: PRINT : PRINT "THIS IS NOT CONSIDERED SIGNIFICANT AS": PRINT : PRINT "AN INDICATION OF PSYCHICAL ABILITIES."

240 REM GIVE OPPORTUNITY OF ANOTHER GO

250 REM IF NOT THEN TERMINATE PROGRAM

260 VTAB 21: PRINT "ANOTHER RUN OF THE CARDS (Y/N)? ";: GET A$: IF A$ < > "Y" AND A$ < > "N" THEN 260

270 IF A$ = "Y" THEN 20

280 END

290 TEXT : HOME : INVERSE : PRINT "RUN NUMBER ";J: NORMAL

300 REM SET UP TEST DISPLAY

310 VTAB 5: PRINT "STAR. . . . . .1": PRINT : PRINT "CROSS. . . . . .2": PRINT : PRINT "WAVY LINES. . . . . . . .3": PRINT : PRINT "SQUARE . . . . .4": PRINT: PRINT "CIRCLE. . . . . .5"

320 VTAB 23: PRINT "ACTUAL CARD SELECTED WILL THEN APPEAR. ": VTAB 20: PRINT "TYPE NUMBER ONLY TO MAKE

```
YOUR GUESS.": GET G: IF G < 1 THEN 320
330 IF G > 5 THEN 320
340 REM RANDOMLY SELECT CARD WHEN GUESS IS MADE
350 R = INT ( RND (1) * 5) + 1
360 HOME
370 VTAB 12: HTAB 15: FLASH
380 REM SHOW CARD SELECTED
390 ON R GOTO 400, 410, 420, 430, 440
400 PRINT "STAR": GOTO 460
410 PRINT "CROSS": GOTO 460
420 PRINT "WAVY LINES": GOTO 460
430 PRINT "SQUARE": GOTO 460
440 PRINT "CIRCLE"
450 REM CALCULATE NUMBER OF CORRECT GUESSES
460 IF G = R THEN TR = TR + 1
470 REM CALCULATE NUMBER OF GUESSES ABOVE CHANCE
EXPECTATION
480 AC = TR − (N * 10): IF AC < 0 THEN AC = 0
490 REM SET FIRST SIGNIFICANT SCORE AS SPECIAL CASE
500 IF AC = 1 THEN PR = 5: GOTO 530
510 REM CALCULATE SUBSEQUENT ODDS AGAINST
CHANCE
520 IF AC = OC + 1 THEN PR = PR * 2
530 NORMAL
540 VTAB 21: INPUT "PRESS <RETURN> TO CONTINUE ":A$:
IF A$ < > " " THEN 540
545 OC = AC
550 REM EXIT SUBROUTINE TO RETURN TO LOOP
560 RETURN
570 REM INSTRUCTIONS SUBROUTINE
580 HOME : PRINT "THIS TEST IS BASED ON E.S.P. RESEARCH":
PRINT : PRINT "CARRIED OUT BY DR J. B. RHINE AT THE
DUKE": PRINT : PRINT "UNIVERSITY OF NORTH CAROLINA":
PRINT
590 PRINT "IT MAKES USE OF SPECIAL SYMBOLIC CARDS":
PRINT : PRINT "KNOWN AS A ZENER PACK.": PRINT : PRINT
"THIS PACK CONTAINS A TOTAL OF 25 CARDS.": PRINT :
```

PRINT "AND FEATURES FIVE DISTINCTIVE SYMBOLS"
600 VTAB 21: INPUT "PRESS <RETURN> FOR ZENER LIST ";A$:
IF A$ < > " " THEN 600
610 HOME : INVERSE
620 VTAB 7
630 HTAB 15: PRINT "STAR"
640 HTAB 15: PRINT "CROSS"
650 HTAB 15: PRINT "WAVY LINES"
660 HTAB 15: PRINT "SQUARE"
670 HTAB 15: PRINT "CIRCLE"
680 NORMAL
690 VTAB 21: PRINT "STAR. .CROSS. .WAVY LINES. .SQUARE. .
CIRCLE": PRINT : INPUT "PRESS<RETURN>WHEN READY";
A$ IF A$< >" "
THEN 690
700 TEXT : HOME : PRINT "IN THE TEST YOU ARE REQUIRED
TO GUESS": PRINT : "WHICH CARDS THE COMPUTER WILL
SELECT. ": PRINT : PRINT "A RUN OF CARDS COMPRISES 25
GUESSES.": PRINT : PRINT "YOU CAN SELECT IN ADVANCE
THE NUMBER OF"
710 PRINT : PRINT "RUNS YOU WISH TO MAKE": PRINT : PRINT
"IT IS WORTH NOTING THAT THE LARGER THE": PRINT
"NUMBER OF RUNS, THE MORE ACCURATE THE": PRINT :
PRINT "RESULTS OF THE TEST."
720 VTAB 21: INPUT "PRESS <RETURN > WHEN READY "; A$:
IF A$ < > " " THEN 720
730 RETURN
740 REM ERROR TRAPPING ROUTINE
750 HOME : VTAB 7: PRINT "ONLY THE ";: INVERSE : PRINT
"NUMBER";: NORMAL : PRINT " SHOULD BE TYPED. PLEASE":
PRINT : PRINT "AVOID ANY OTHER KEY AND DO NOT USE
THE": PRINT : PRINT "<RETURN> KEY HERE.
760 VTAB 15: PRINT "FOR ACCURACY OF EVALUATION WE'LL
START": PRINT : PRINT "THE TEST AGAIN.": PRINT : INPUT
"PRESS <RETURN> WHEN READY ";A$: IF A$< >" " THEN
760
770 HOME : GOTO 110

That's the listing in Applesoft. Users of a different BASIC dialect should have little trouble in converting if they pay attention to the following points:

LINE 40: This directs the program to an error trapping subroutine at Line 750. If your BASIC does not have the ONERR command, this line and lines 750 to 770 may simply be omitted.

LINE 60: Here and elsewhere the VTAB and HTAB commands are convenient in the layout of the display. VTAB sets the vertical line position. HTAB sets the horizontal position of the cursor. Substitute commands from your own BASIC may be used here; or alternatively you can always redesign the displays to suit your own taste.

LINE 80: The HOME command here and elsewhere in the program clears the Apple screen and sets the cursor to the top left hand corner of the screen. You may have to substitute CLS or some similar command from your own BASIC.

LINE 110: INVERSE here and elsewhere instructs the computer to display the subsequent PRINT lines black on white. It is cancelled by the next NORMAL command. Here again you can substitute or simply change the display to suit your own taste.

LINE 220: FLASH causes the next print command to be displayed in flashing mode. Like INVERSE this command is cancelled by NORMAL. Substitute or change to suit yourself.

LINE 350: This code generates a random number in the range 1 to 5. Use the substitute random number generation sequence from your own BASIC.

LINE 390: If your BASIC lacks the ON . . . GOTO command, you may substitute a series of IF . . . THEN lines. (IF R = 1 THEN <LINE NUMBER> etc.)

LINE 540: Here and elsewhere, pressing the <RETURN> key generates a null string input. You may substitute any coding which allows the user to take control of the program at these points.

When it runs, this program will first ask you, or the subject you are testing, whether you need instructions. If your answer is "Y" for yes, then some background on the test will be displayed and a brief indication given as to how it runs.

Since instructions are seldom necessary after the first time, the answer "N" for no will take you directly into the test itself.

In the test itself, your first decision is how may runs of the cards you want to try. Each run permits you to guess 25 cards in all, so two runs gives 50 guesses, three runs 75 guesses and so on. While you have a better chance of getting a psi score in a small number of runs, the result is usually a little spurious. Strictly speaking, you can only really rely on the test if you make a minimum of four runs at a single sitting.

On the other hand, if you consistently show a psi score over an even longer number of runs, you may congratulate yourself on having become a psi star, since the test is remarkably accurate in such situations.

While presented as a generic ESP test, this program actually tests primarily for precognitive talent since the selected card is not generated until *after* you have made your guess. (Only a split second after, but that does not negate the point). Because of this, it may be useful to you to attempt some of the other psi tests (telepathy), etc given in the next chapter.

Finally, it is as well to mention that if early attempts at this or any other test show no psi ability, you should not become discouraged. Just like any other talent or ability, ESP can almost always be developed and improved with practice: and you will find ample ways to practice throughout the remainder of this book. Furthermore, when you come to your experiments in a Batcheldor-style group, it is as well to realize clearly that Batcheldor emphasizes that psi ability is *not* necessary for success.

16

The Psychic Deck

For those without a home computer, ESP testing remains perfectly possible. Zener packs are available commercially from a number of specialist outlets and they will normally come complete with instructions on how to set up your own experiments.

If, however, you cannot get hold of a Zener pack (or are just too impatient to try!) you can substitute an ordinary deck of playing cards without too much loss of accuracy in the final evaluation.

As mentioned earlier, scientists have long abandoned the use of playing cards because psychological reactions to certain of them tend to influence the data being collected. But while results obtained with playing cards cannot be accepted as *scientifically* valid, they can certainly give a useful indication of psi talent for all practical purposes.

Playing cards and one or two interested helpers will, in fact, allow you to test for psi on a much broader base than the computer program given in the last chapter. And even if you are working entirely alone, you can still produce interesting results. There are, however, a few areas common to all the experiments which require special attention.

The first is the cards themselves. Use a new deck if at all possible; and if you are engaged in a lengthy run of experimentation, change to a new deck frequently. Well-used cards pick up markings (bent corners, specks of dirt and so on) which may be used unconsciously as clues to their value. In statistical analysis, knowledge of even one card in 52 can throw the calculations badly out of gear.

The second area to watch is the note-taking. In any experiment, you are going to have to make a note of the number of correct guesses. This sounds simple enough, but it is a psychological minefield. Painstaking research has shown conclusively that here again the Sheep and Goats Syndrome has a distinct tendency to rear its head. If you believe in the possibility of ESP, there is an excellent chance you will begin (quite unconsciously, of course) to record correct guesses that never happened. If you are a confirmed sceptic, then (again unconsciously) you will tend to 'forget' to note one or two correct guesses.

Please resist the temptation to conclude that this could not happen to you. The unconscious mind is a strange animal and those tendencies definitely exist. Furthermore, it only needs a few mistakes of this kind to invalidate your entire body of results.

The final area for close attention is the calculation of the odds. Here too, your unconscious will pressurize you to make a Sheep or Goat mistake. To cut down on the possibility, I have included probability tables in this chapter so the difficult calculations are all done for you. But even this method is by no means foolproof — you may be driven into mistakes in looking up the tables!

The only sure answer to this problem is to take special care in both areas — and, having taken special care, to recheck and, if necessary, recheck again. It may seem a tortuous procedure, but it is absolutely necessary.

Discounting any Jokers which may be around, your deck has 52 cards divided into four suits — spades, hearts, diamonds, clubs. The suits are themselves divided into two: black cards (spades and clubs) and red cards (hearts and diamonds). Within the suits there is a further subdivision of Court cards (King, Queen, Jack or Knave and usually Ace) and suit cards (2 to 10). Any or all of these subdivisions may be pressed into service as a psi test.

Let's begin with something simple. Take your deck and shuffle it well. Place it face down on the table in front of you. Take a notepad and pencil and write down whether you think the top card is red or black. Now the next card down — red or black? Now

the next . . . and the next . . . and so on until you have made
52 guesses in all. At this point, you should not have touched
the actual deck since the time you shuffled and laid it on the
table.

Now take the top card from the deck, turn it over and check
(carefully!) whether or not your guess was correct. Make a note
in your pad of the actual colour and also whether or not you
were right. Repeat the process until you have checked the entire
deck.

Since any given card has to be either red or black, you have
a 50/50 chance of being correct every time you make a guess. Over
the run of the pack, this means you will correctly guess 26 cards
(52 divided by 2) on the basis of chance alone. If, however, you
find you have guessed *more than* 26 cards correctly, (or, indeed,
less than 26 cards correctly) you have produced a *deviation from
chance.*

If the deviation is only one or two cards, it is unlikely to be
very significant — especially over a single run of the deck. But
if the deviation is more pronounced, it may include psi talent.
Check the tables at the end of this chapter to find the odds against
your deviation. The higher they run, the more chance there is
that you are using psi.

In this, as in all the experiments outlined, deviations that show
consistently over long runs of the cards are more significant than
those showing in short runs.

Although simple to execute, it is not a particularly good idea
to concentrate exclusively on colour guessing. The bane of all
psychical research is the boredom level of participants. It has been
shown conclusively that the performance of even star subjects
tends to fall away dramatically if the subject becomes bored. For
this reason, variety in testing is important, as is the concept of
reward.

In your case, the reward may have to be self-supplied. But it
should not be neglected on this account. Decide in advance of
any test that you are going to treat yourself to something pleasant
in the event of a positive psi score. This may be nothing more
than a chocolate from the box, a good cigar or another chapter

from the thriller you are enjoying. You know what you like, so you pick the reward. But enjoy the reward if you succeed and deny yourself the reward if you fail. It may seem a small enough thing, but it can make a great deal of difference to your score.

As a variation on colour guessing, you may follow the same procedure as before, but this time attempt to guess the *suit* of each card. Here the odds are four to one against a hit, so that on the complete run of the deck, your chance expectation is 13. Again the tables will indicate the chance odds against any significant deviation from this score.

When you have tired of suit guessing, move on to guessing the actual card. Remember that you should not check your guesses as you go along — to do so would tell you what cards have been removed from the deck and hence invalidate any score you may achieve. Odds against a correct guess in this experiment are quite high — 52 to 1. So any score above one represents a deviation. Again, you should use the tables to find out the degree of significance your score represents.

All these experiments will test for *either* precognition or clairvoyance. As they are presently structured, it is impossible to determine which of the two talents has begun to manifest. You may, however, change the structure with the help of a partner; and in doing so, determine in which area your talent lies.

In the new versions of the experiments, your partner is responsible for shuffling the deck and checking what results, if any, you achieved from your guesswork. If you decide in advance of a given run that your partner will tell you only the *result* of the experiment without indicating in any way which cards you actually guessed correctly, then you have tested for clairvoyance and not precognition. If, on the other hand, the experiment ends with your being told the actual run of the cards, the chances are that you are showing precognition with a positive score (although it has to be admitted that clairvoyance cannot be absolutely ruled out).

Having obtained a partner, you may as well go on to test for telepathy. The simplest method is for you to sit back-to-back. One of you turns over the cards from a shuffled deck one at a time and concentrates on it, trying to visualize the card clearly in his mind's eye. The other attempts to guess what card is currently being viewed. As before, each guess is written down without comment and, as before, evaluation is made after the experiment has been completed by comparing the written guesses with the actual run of the deck.

You may vary these tests by guessing Red or Black, guessing suit or guessing the actual card. In all cases the same probabilities apply as they did in your solitary experiments, so you can use the same tables to evaluate your deviations.

Just as there are natural Sheep and Goats, so there are natural 'senders' and 'receivers', so that it may be useful if you and your partner switch roles after a few runs in order to clarify where your natural aptitudes may lie.

If you begin to achieve positive results in these experiments, it could be interesting to tighten up your test procedure. As outlined, even in a back-to-back situation, there are opportunities for unconscious signals to pass between you and your partner. These can be as subtle as changes in voice inflection, but subtle or not, there remains a very real possibility that your sneaky old unconscious mind may pick them up and use them to produce inaccurate results.

Tightening up test procedure will involve calling in a third party to run the next experiments, which should take place with sender and receiver in different rooms — if feasible, even in different buildings. Don't be too disappointed if this move depresses the ultimate psi score. Almost certainly it will, but equally certainly the results you *do* achieve will be far more evidential. And remember too the Batcheldor Effect. Tightening up procedures invariably lessened PK manifestations until the sitters became accustomed to the new situation. In psi, self-confidence is everything.

Probability Tables

Colour Guessing

Your chance score on a run of 52 cards is 26. This figure doubles
on two consecutive runs, trebles on three, etc. Find the number
of correct guesses you made *above* chance score and the table
shows you the odds in favour of your having used psi.

Scored above chance	Psi odds to 1
1	Even
2	2
3	4
4	8
5	16
6	32
7	64
8	128
9	256
10	512
11	1024
12	2048
13	4096
14	8192
15	16384
16	32768
17	65536
18	131072
19	262144
20	524288
21	1048576
22	2097152
23	4194304
24	8388608
25	16777216
26	33554432

Suit Guessing

Your chance score on a run of 52 cards is 13.

Scored above chance	Psi odds to 1
1	4
2	8
3	16
4	32
5	64
6	128
7	256
8	512
9	1024
10	2048
11	4096
12	8192
13	16384
14	32768
15	65536
17	131072
18	262144
19	524288
20	1048576
21	2097152
22	4194304
23	8388608
24	16777216
25	33554432
26	67108864
27	134217728
28	268435456

Note: Chances of psi arising out of higher deviation run into billions.

Card Guessing

Chance will give you 1 correct guess in a run of 52 cards.

Scored above chance	Psi odds to 1
1	·52
2	104
3	208
4	416
5	832
6	1664
7	3328
8	6656
9	13312
10	26624
11	53248
12	106496
13	212992
14	425984
15	851968
16	1703936
17	3407872
18	6815744
19	13631488
20	27263976
21	54525952
22	109051904
23	218103808
24	436207616
25	872415232

Note: Higher scores involve psi odds in the billions.

17
PK Testing

It is not possible to test for PK using cards — unless, of course, your talent has developed to such a degree that you can hurl them around the room like a poltergeist.

But PK can be tested; and one of the most spectacular tests involves no more elaborate equipment than a cork, a needle and a square of lightweight silver paper of the type found inside almost any cigarette packet.

To set up your apparatus, first separate the silver paper from its tissue backing (no easy task, but possible if you persevere). There are generally two separate pieces of this paper in British cigarette packs: one which wraps around the cigarettes themselves, the other which is placed at the top and thrown away when the smoker extracts his first cigarette. It is this latter piece you need since the size is about right for your purpose.

Take this piece and, having separated the backing, fold and cut it so you are left with a square. Now crease the square along its diagonals; and again by folding top to bottom and side to side. If you have done it properly, the creases will form this pattern:

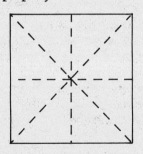

Now fold again, using the creases as guidelines, so you end up with a little tent.

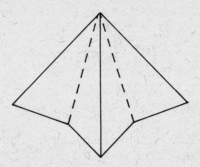

Leave your little tent to one side. Take your needle and embed it in the cork so that it forms an upright metal shaft. Now place the silver paper tent on top of the needle.

What you have created is a miniature mobile. The silver paper tent is so finely balanced that it will (or should!) spin freely when the slightest force is applied to it. That force will, hopefully, originate in your mind.

To test for PK, set up your little apparatus on the table in front of you, checking carefully that it is out of the way of draughts. Now sit a few feet away and concentrate on spinning the silver tent.

How you try to do this is really up to you — if there are firm rules to the operation of psychokinesis, science has not yet found them. But there are indications that visualization may help. Try to form a picture in your mind's eye of the tent beginning to spin, then moving faster and faster until it is racing around like a merry-go-round.

If you are lucky — the PK active — you will first notice small movements in the tent, rather like tiny involunary muscle twitches. After this, the tent will begin to spin.

Although the spinning tent is a fun experiment to attempt, it can take quite a lot of time and effort before any results appear; and for some people they never appear at all. Thus it is quite important to have a standby PK test which will give a much more measurable reading of your development. Fortunately this is easily achieved using the statistical approach developed by Rhine. The only equipment you need is a set of dice.

You can increase the validity of your methodology by selecting your dice with care. An ordinary die is a cube, usually of wood or plastic, with spots showing on each of its six sides. The number of spots on opposite sides always adds up to seven. It is tempting to imagine that, given such a simple arrangement, one die is much the same as any other. But this is not actually the case. Virtually all commercially produced dies show a slight statistical bias. This is not strong enough to affect your game of Snakes and Ladders, but it can influence the end result of any PK test.

The reason for the bias is not difficult to see once you begin to think about it. A perfect cube, when rolled, will fall randomly with consistent 6 to 1 odds against any particular side ending up on top. But this is a perfect cube *without* the spots which turn it into a dice.

Manufacturers add die spots in one of two ways. They may be painted or embossed on the sides; or they may be cut into the sides. Either method produces a bias, although in different directions.

When you paint a single spot on the side of a cube, you add weight to that side of the cube — the weight of the paint you use. This weight is extremely small, but it still represents a real quantum. More to the point, when you paint six spots on a side, you add six times the weight of paint that you did when you painted one.

In statistical terms, this means there will always be a very slight tendency for a painted dice to fall showing a score of one. The one-spot is the lightest of all six sides, thus it has a tiny statistical tendency to end up on top.

Cutting the spots into the sides of the cube produces the same problem in reverse. Cutting spots extracts material from a given side, making it lighter. In a cut die, the six-spot side is the lightest, since it has the most material removed. Thus, again, on a statistical basis, this side shows a slight tendency to end up on top.

Of the three types of widely available dice, cut dice are least suitable for your experiments, since the bias is the most pronounced. Embossed dice (where the painted spots are raised from the surface of the cube) are almost as bad. While not perfect, straightforward painted dice are probably your best bet. Some manufacturers produce dice in plastic where the spots are shown by colouring within the plastic itself, not painted, embossed or cut in afterwards. This type of dye shows no bias whatsoever and is ideal for your purpose . . . if you can find it.

Once you have your die, testing yourself for PK is easy, although to do it properly, you will need the help of a friend. Have him throw the die using a cup in such a way that you cannot see the result. Your job is to concentrate on making that die come up six every time.

You are unlikely to succeed in your endeavour, but you may well succeed in producing a statistical bias towards a six roll and the odds against this bias can be evaluated exactly like those of the card-calling experiments outlined in the last chapter.

Your friend should take careful note of the sixes which actually appeared. For your own convenience, work in sequences of thirty six rolls. A single sequence will give you chance expectation of six sixes. Anything above or below this is a deviation. Use the following table to determine the odds in favour of a PK element having arisen.

Scored above chance	*PK odds to 1*
1	6
2	12
3	24
4	48
5	96
6	192
7	384
8	768
9	1536
10	3072
11	6144
12	12288
13	24576
14	49152
15	98304
16	196608
17	393216
18	786432
19	1572864
20	3145728
21	6291456
22	12582912
23	25165824
24	50331648
25	100663296
26	201326592
27	402653184
28	805306368
29	1.61061274E+09
30	3.22122547E+09

The last two figures, given in scientific notation, indicate astronomical chances in favour of PK. But to achieve them, you will have to cause the die to show a six almost consistently throughout the entire run.

It is worth noting that you can conduct this test yourself,

without the aid of a helper, but in doing so, it becomes impossible to determine whether you are using PK or precognition if a positive score results.

18

Starting a B-Group

There is a theory that the use of psychical abilities tends to improve them, as exercise will improve the performance of a muscle. Although there is some anthropological evidence to support this, experience shows it does not readily hold true for statistical tests — the boredom factor tends eventually to overwhelm even the most carefully structured system of rewards.

To improve your mindreach to any significant degree, a new approach is needed: and it is such an approach which Kenneth Batcheldor has provided in his experiments with gross PK.

As we have seen, Batcheldor's method involves a working group, and group psychology differs significantly from personal psychology, even when the individual concerned is a member of the group. The inner dynamics are different, so that while boredom can arise in the group context, it does not arise often when experiments are properly structured. More to the point, group activities often generate their own momentum.

How then can you go about setting up a Batcheldor style group — a B-group as I now propose to call it?

When he was involved in his earlier experiments, Batcheldor suspected his own group had a medium in their midst. Later, he swung away from this notion and while the influence of mediumistic talents in these experiments must remain an open question, it now seems evident that virtually any dedicated group has the potential of producing results, whether it contains a specially talented individual or not. This is good news for anyone planning to set up a B-group. It opens up the choice of sitters dramatically. In theory, anyone willing to join could join. In practice, however, it will pay you to be a little more selective.

It could be useful to think for a moment about groups in general — amateur drama circles, political movements, craft workshops, Masonic Lodges and the like — and ask yourself what makes for the smooth operation of those of them which succeed.

The 'glue' that holds any group together is mutual interest. This is an obvious statement, but one which bears closer examination. When you start to think about it, not everyone joins a dramatic society because they are interested in stagecraft. The real motive might be social — a desire to make new friends. Or something to do in the evenings. Or a crush on the leading lady. Or the hope of making business contacts. And so on.

There is, of course, nothing wrong with any of these motivations. But experience will confirm they do not serve the central purpose of the group particularly well. A drama circle is at its best when it is composed entirely of single-minded, dedicated members. Standards drop in direct proportion to the number of those members who joined for reasons other than a love of the stage.

The same thing holds good for a group engaged in psychical research and the generation of PK phenomena. As you cast around for suitable individuals, you may be sure of attracting the interest of several who would do better in a glee club. Their expressed motives may sound excellent, but their real motives may be at considerable variance. Drama groups are usually large enough to be able to absorb quite a few members with only marginal real interest in the stage. A workable B-group is too small for such luxuries. But there is a simple answer to the problem: pick your members with care.

Common sense is an excellent guide here. You will obviously be looking for members with an interest in psychical matters. They must have sufficient free time to devote to the experiments *on a regular basis*. A track record for staying power could be useful.

Try to avoid personality conflicts in your selection. It is easy enough to avoid inviting known enemies to join, but the most troublesome personality conflicts tend to be more subtle. You can do without individuals who only want to amuse their colleagues, cynics determined to explain away everything that happens, cranks seeking confirmation of their personal beliefs.

Hard experience taught Batcheldor not to underestimate the problems. In a monograph of practical hints for group formation he had this to say: 'It seems difficult to find a number of people of suitable outlook who are both willing and able to meet regularly. There may be little choice among one's acquaintances. Occasionally the wife or husband of an interested person may have to be included, or other less motivated persons.'

If possible, he suggests, sitters should be open-minded, calm, friendly, willing to co-operate with the group leader and above all patient. Patience may actually be the prime consideration. Members must be prepared if necessary to sit for hours with nothing more than simple table movements happening – and to keep this up for several weeks on end. Although many B-groups obtain their first results early enough, Batcheldor advises striking an initial bargain with members to try the system, come what may, for a minimum of ten weeks before abandoning it.

Your group will have a better chance of success if it is composed wholly, or largely, of those who believe PK to be a real possibility. Central to the Batcheldor theories is the concept that mindset influences results. If the dominant mindset of your group is that PK is impossible, then results become extremely difficult to achieve.

But Batcheldor has a caveat on this point. He advises against the inclusion of convinced and practising Spiritualists. Although accustomed to witnessing quite dramatic seance room displays, such individuals, he feels, are often psychologically incapable of discarding the Spiritualist explanation of psychical phenomena, and this interferes with experiments structured to display PK as a human skill.

While no wild talents seem to be necessary for sitters, a few tame talents may prove extemely useful. Batcheldor (a psychologist) was helped in the construction of instruments by Brookes-Smith (an engineer). Once you begin to consider the structure of your experiments, you will begin to see the sort of expertise which could be helpful. Engineers may be relied on to produce the sort of devices necessary to establish controlled conditions. Photographers could be valuable to record some of the more spectacular visual results. Trained observers — journalists, police officers, scientists, etc. — will make the best witnesses. And so on.

Here again you are likely to achieve the perfect mix, but you can at least try to create the most effective group your particular circumstances and contacts allow, although Batcheldor would warn against introducing any apparatus, photography or controls too soon in the series of sittings.

How many sitters will you need? Batcheldor remarks that it is probably possible to obtain results with any number of sitters from one upwards. But experience suggests that less then three is unfavourable. 'Three or more persons lend one another moral support and help reduce the factor of emotional resistance', he says.

But there is another, even more important, consideration here, related to the technical process of the experiments themselves. Once table movements are detected, there is an understandable human impulse to test the phenomenon (by, for example, pushing against the movement or removing one's hands from the table). When this occurs, groups of three or more tend to keep the table in motion.

If three is a workng minimum of sitters, six seems to be a good maximum to aim for. Larger groups are physically awkward and will besides invite the conclusion that any movement of the table arises from the sitters' unconscious muscle movements. They also create more problems with harmonious sittings and regular attendance.

Once you have chosen your group, it is as well to avoid bringing in new members. If Batcheldor's theories are correct, you are really embarking on a process of group conditioning. Newcomers, however suitable they might be, are almost always a disruptive influence on this process. For the same reason, changes of venue should be avoided; and even changes within the venue. The only real exception are situations in which certain individuals prove disruptive or the group has not succeeded after many weeks. (Obviously *some* changes will be unavoidable. Sooner or later you will want to introduce controls on your experiments, for example. In such situations, Batcheldor suggests the changes are introduced as gradually as possible only after strong results have been regularly obtained – and warns that even then they will have an adverse effect on results until the sitters become well accustomed to them.)

With your group established, your next job is to find a suitable place to meet. Obviously, it should be somewhere convenient to your sitters, but avoid the temptation of rotating the meeting place to suit various members, since this approach introduces change. Find a good central location and stick to it.

Ideally, you will need somewhere where you can conduct your experiments free from the possibility of disturbance. But it is as well to remember that disturbance works both ways. A successful PK session can become an extremely noisy affair and neighbours generally do not take kindly to things that go bump in the night. If you have thin walls, a little soundproofing will go a long way.

Although the chances are that your group will meet in the evenings, you should make sure you have some means of excluding light. Shutters are ideal, but failing these, heavy curtaining must be provided. Check too that you have sufficient power points to run any equipment you might decide to use.

Finally, decide on how often your group will meet. Once a week will probably prove convenient for most sitters. Twice a week is about the maximum you should reasonably aim for. More frequent meetings tend to exhaust sitters and are actually counterproductive in terms of results. Length of any given session should be a minimum of one hour. Batcheldor suggests two-hour sessions with a break half-way through and warns that meetings should never be prolonged beyond the point where sitters become tired, bored or disheartened. It is a good idea to begin meetings at the same time on the same day of each week.

19
Preparing for PK

With your group established and a meeting place arranged, you can turn your attention to your preparations for an actual session. The first and most obvious thing you will have to do is find a table.

This innocent item of furniture, which will be the focus of much of your activities, can theoretically be of any shape, size and material that takes your fancy. But here again, practice differs.

At the risk of repetition, belief is the necessary ingredient for PK sessions and much of the Batcheldor methodology is structured towards the creation of an environment in which belief tends progressively to strengthen. We have already seen that even Rhine's most gifted subjects disliked working with lead dice. In the context of your own group, new sitters faced, for example, with a Victorian banquet table in heavy mahogany might be forgiven for concluding that a team of workmen would have difficulty moving it, let alone a group of sitters using only their mental concentration. So don't choose too heavy a table, at least not to begin with. Later, with practice, you will be able to influence much heavier tables.

You should remember too that there is an excellent chance any table you use may end up damaged or broken, so avoid choosing a priceless antique. (And on this point, it is good insurance to move any valuable ornaments out of the room as well!)

In the early stages of your experiments, any table movements will almost certainly result from unconscious muscle movements. But precisely because they *are* caused unconsciously, such movements will seem impressive to sitters and thus tend to reinforce belief that PK is possible. Consequently, your table should be light enough to ensure that movements due to unconscious muscle action do occur at a reasonably early stage.

But there is a subtle trap here. If the table is *too* light, sitters may be tempted to conclude that *all* movements can be explained in this way. Batcheldor's experience suggests the best compromise is a table weighing 4 lbs per sitter present. Thus a group of three should work with a 12 lb table, a group of four with a 16 lb table, and so on.

This is not, however, an absolute requirement, but rather something that is relative to the shape of the table. It is often easier to quantify unconscious muscle action by measuring the horizontal force needed to tip a table rather than the force necessary to lift it as deadweight. But the horizontal force will vary greatly in relation to table shape: a tall, narrow table is obviously easier to tilt than a short squat one of the same weight. If horizontal force is taken as the criterion, Batcheldor suggests starting at ½ lb to 1 lb per person, irrespective of actual table weight, and increasing this gradually at a later stage.

The type of table you use is probably not critical. Tradition calls for a wooden table without major metal components, but most tables fall into this category in any case. Batcheldor recommends a cheap table with reinforced joints, kept specially for the experiments so that equipment may be screwed onto it if necessary. Do not worry if it creaks a little when moved. Indeed this can prove a good thing, since experience shows noises of this sort, in the right context, can actually encourage the development of genuine PK.

Apart from the table, the only other piece of equipment you will need to get started is a tape recorder. Although not absolutely essential, a good machine would be a worthwhile investment. You will have to keep some sort of record of your experiments and simple note-taking is not really recommended since mistaken perceptions can all too easily falsify the report. A tape recorder, on the other hand, is impartial, easy to operate and extremely useful.

Batcheldor used a reel-to-reel machine originally — he found a two-hour meeting just filled a 1,200 ft spool running at 3¾ inches per second. But the larger recorders of this type are usually expensive, so that you may prefer a cassette machine. Fortunately, these little recorders are now generally quite reliable and the best of them are extremely sensitive. The main problem is recording time. The longest-running commercial cassette (a C120) will give only one hour's recording time per side, so that the cassette must be turned over at that time. If you follow Batcheldor's plan of a two-hour meeting with a break half-way though, this may not prove too troublesome, but my personal experience has been that many C120 tapes are unreliable, especially after a few uses. The C60 and C90 cassettes give greater technical reliability, but less recording time per side (30 and 45 minutes respectively).

With a weather eye out for anything which might disturb the sitters, Batcheldor recommends placing the recorder outside the room and using a long lead to suspend the microphone from the ceiling about four feet above the table. This is not necessary if you use a cassette recorder, but any pilot lights should be covered over.

In any event, you should begin each session by recording all the relevant details of the experiment – date, place, time, names and positions of sitters, lighting conditions, size, shape and weight of table and any special apparatus in use. Once your experiments are finished, you can prepare written records from your tapes.

There are, of course, more elaborate methods of keeping track of any phenomena which may occur. Batcheldor mentions the use of infra-red video-recording – which may not be quite so exotic as it sounds, given the widespread proliferation of home video systems over the past few years. But it is probably as well to keep your more spectacular technical arrangements for a later stage of the experiments. The beginning is a particularly sensitive time and the less novelty you present to your sitters the better.

Your next decision will be what to do about lighting. There is a strong tradition that light interferes with psychical phenomena, and there is no doubt that this is true, especially in the early stages of their development.

But as we have already noted, Batcheldor considers that it is not light that causes the trouble, but sight — or, more accurately, the thoughts of the observers.

Whatever the reason, maximum progress is likely by making the room as dark as possible (although a small luminous marker in the middle of the table might be permitted). A good rule of thumb to adopt is that if you can still see the sitters' hands on the table, your room is not dark enough.

While simple movements with contact, and even raps, can be produced in light, Batcheldor's experience has been that it is extremely difficult to develop levitations and movements without contact in anything other than darkness. *After* they have been developed in this way and strengthened by repetition, it is sometimes possible gradually to introduce a little light — preferably red light.

If your sitters are nervous in total darkness, start with as low a lighting level as they will accept — a door slightly ajar with a light outside for example — then move on to total darkness as soon as you can. Most people become accustomed to this regime very quickly, although it is a good idea for you to keep a torch in your pocket and make plain that you will switch it on at once should any sitter call for it.

Quite obviously, sitting in total darkness makes the detection of fraud more difficult. But according to Batcheldor, this is a necessary limitation if good results are to be obtained within a reasonable time. The elusive quality of spectacular PK is a fact that has to be accepted. It is simply not possible to obtain results that are both strong and clearly visible at one and the same time. If you insist on sitting in light from the start, your phenomena will almost certainly be weak.

If, at a much later stage, you decide to experiment with weak light, red is usually favoured, though it can be tiring on the eyes. According to Batcheldor, red light probably works best because it is more difficult to see detail under red light than under almost any other colour. But any colour of light should work, provided it is dim enough to prevent clear perception of detail.

A variable light source can be provided by using a boxed light set facing a wall. It only requires to move the box further from the wall to increase the overall lighting level.

Batcheldor makes the ingenious suggestion that the light might actually be controlled by table movements. A gravity-operated pendulum switch attached to the table can operate a light should the table tilt. But since tilts are normally possible in full light, a better approach might be to set up a small red bulb which lights only when all of four switches on the feet of the table are released — in other words, a total levitation. Here again, light level should be kept very low at first and only increased gradually as the experiment series proceeds. Batcheldor's group was able eventually to exchange the red light for a white one. But he does caution that devices of this sort should be kept firmly switched off until a number of levitations have been achieved without them.

Sessions held in total darkness can be extremely difficult to evaluate since individual perceptions of what is actually happening vary dramatically. A good standby in this respect is the old Spiritualist trick of using luminous paint to mark the table or any other object which may be used. You can avoid painting the objects themselves by using sticky labels which have been previously marked with a very small dab of luminous paint. Coat them with clear nail varnish to prolong their life and refresh the paint at the beginning of each session by exposing it to a strong light source. Avoid marking the sitters, however, as this introduces a partial control against fraud and thus affects the mindset.

Finally, at this stage, it is as well to note that phenomena other than PK might arise in the course of your experiments. Batcheldor has some interesting comments on this and it may be useful to quote him in full:

> The unsophisticated usually report many unfamiliar sensations, mainly resulting from suggestion and increased attention to the body, or to small sounds or lights which would normally pass unnoticed.

If attention is directed over a period of time by most sitters to one of these areas, genuine phenomena appropriate to the area of attention may develop.

For example, by listening to creaks and taps in the table, genuine raps may begin to occur. This is not an illusion. One gets the phenomena which one sits for or pays attention to — though this is only true if the anticipated phenomena are plausible and the psi state (i.e. an expectant atmosphere) is adequate and there is freedom from resistance and effort.

If a new phenomenon is attended to, the one going on previously tends to stop. We once became interested in breezes, which eventually increased to a minor whirlwind; meantime all table movements stopped.

Any new phenomenon develops gradually — everything is always gradual. If table movements are the main aim, attention should be kept on these; otherwise their development will be held up by the development of different phenomena — breezes, lights, touchings, raps and possibly other more advanced phenomena such as apports.

On which exciting note it is now time to describe how to conduct your first meeting!

20
Your First Meeting

With your group assembled and your preparations complete, the time at last arrives for your first meeting. It is likely that your sitters will be a little nervous — and even more likely that you will be a little nervous yourself! Take time to relax and explain, as far as possible, what will be going on. In particular, allow your sitters to make themselves at home and examine the table, chairs, room and any pieces of special equipment you may be using. Background music may be played if this helps the atmosphere, although this should be as low volume as possible so that any sounds from the table can be clearly descerned.

The table is placed in the centre of the room and your group will take their places around it. Allow them to work out any order of seating which suits them best. Some groups advocate segregating the sexes, others alternate them, but there is no hard and fast ruling except that the sitters themselves should feel comfortable with the final arrangements. Once the seating order has been established, however, make sure that it remains the same for all subsequent meetings. Even small changes in the routine, as Batcheldor has often stressed, are counterproductive in the generation of phenomena.

Each sitter should place both hands, palms downwards, on the surface of the table with their wrists roughly at the edge. Once everyone is in position, the recorder started and the lights lowered (or switched off altogether), you may tell them that the first sign of anything happening is likely to be a series of creaks, possibly followed by a slight movement of the table. After this the waiting starts.

During the waiting period, your sitters may choose to remain silent, but there is certainly no harm in conversation, so long as it is kept *light*. (Remember that the Toronto group who created the fictional ghost Philip only really began to get results when they relaxed, joked and even sang at sessions.)

While there is no substitute for simple patience, a couple of techniques have been discovered which may help stimulate phenomena earlier on than they might otherwise arise.

The first is the so-called Exeter Method. Sitters agree at the outset that they will push and pull the table quite consciously for a period of ten to fifteen seconds in order to produce tilts. Then, while this is going on, each individual sitter decides in his or her own time to stop the conscious effort (although hands should remain in contact with the table). No one mentions that they have stopped consciously influencing the table; and each makes an effort not to speculate on whether the others have stopped. Using this method, the table will normally begin to tilt of its own accord (in reality probably due to unconscious muscle action) after about a minute.

The second method is the Daventry Technique, which was discovered accidentally. The table chosen was unsteady. (It was badly made and the legs were of different lengths.) Very shortly after the sitting began, a rocking motion started up; but, curiously, the table would halt this motion instantly if commanded to do so. The early table movements proved an excellent warm-up for successful sessions. If you are unable to find a badly made table, a little work with a saw will soon convert the table you have into a rocker of this type.

I should mention that while I have personally found both these methods useful, Batcheldor no longer recommends them. In view of this, it may be as well to try the patient approach first, and only if this fails should the Exeter or Daventry methods be adopted.

How long should the waiting period last? Half an hour to an hour is probably long enough before breaking for refreshment and trying again. For your first meeting at least, if nothing has happened over an hour and a half, you should call it a day and arrange the next meeting.

Willing the table to move during the waiting period is unlikely to produce results. Indeed, it is quite likely to inhibit them. Do not try to *do* anything — that would be using the wrong part of your mind. The best mental state seems to be a sort of effortless calm, with no striving for results of any kind. Generally speaking, there is nothing your sitters can do until after the first movement has manifested; and at that point, it is often the table that will take the lead!

But while it is sensible to stress the need for patience, it is equally important to recognize that the group's patience will certainly be rewarded. When the first movement of the table does occur, it is as well for you to know how to deal with it.

Interestingly, that first slide or tilt is most likely to occur when you least expect it. Batcheldor mentions that it typically occurs during a burst of laughter or some other distraction. When it happens, you as leader or spokesperson should discourage analysis or discussion and suggest a calm, blank-minded waiting period for further developments. (Once a movement has been experienced, there is a temptation to try to order the table to move from then on. This should be resisted in the early stages of your experiments and the phenomena allowed to develop naturally at its own pace.) You can encourage it to *increase* whatever it is already doing, but don't give specific commands — and don't try to command anything more advanced. Later on, but only after levitations and not mere tiltings have occurred, it may be interesting, and perhaps even important, to direct the table movements by spoken command. But it is vital to realize that if commands are used too early, the atmosphere will suffer and levitations and other advanced phenomenon may never occur.

It may be as well at this stage to mention that once a particular individual has volunteered or been elected to the position of spokesperson, that person should remain 'in office' for the rest of the experimental series. Here again, we are establishing familiarity and avoiding anything which tends to deviate from familiar patterns. For the same reason, commands given by the spokesperson should not be varied. There are always several possible ways of saying the same thing, but in this context you should pick one of them and stick to it.

Initial movements, while quite definite, are unlikely to be spectacular. But they will gradually increase, both in strength and variety.

Do not push initial successes too far. No attempt at levitations should be made during your first meeting, nor should you try for movements without hand contact. You are embarking on a self-conditioning process and long-term success can only be assured by a gradual approach. For the same reason, you should avoid discussions (or arguments!) about whether the table is being pushed, and also avoid any measurements or scientific testing at this stage. Welcome whatever movements the table is making and encourage them to increase.

While avoiding tests may be simple enough, avoiding argument or discussion is often easier said than done — especially if the table movements are in any way impressive. Your sitters will be very prone to accusing one another of pushing and may actually begin to concentrate their attention on one individual who is chosen as being the most likely 'cheat'. The psychologist Batcheldor refers to this development as 'scape-goating' and links it to a resistance by your sitters to the idea that the table movements may be paranormal. Scape-goating provides the badly needed 'rational' explanation.

As the phenomena continue, scape-goating will not necessarily fade away, although it may well change in character, with the former 'cheat' now being seen as the 'psychic' or 'medium'. While Batcheldor now feels such descriptions are unlikely to be accurate, he advises against taking any direct action against scape-goating in either of its forms. His experience is that a more effective group will develop if scape-goating is allowed to run its course and the sitters form their own conclusions about its ultimate validity.

After a few meetings, if all goes well, substantial (hands-on) table movements should be occurring almost as a matter of course. At this stage the table will seem to be taking on a life of its own — its movements not apparently corresponding to anything the sitters are consciously thinking. When this happens, it is extremely easy for the idea to spring up that the movements are directed by some discamate intelligence separate from the group.

This can create a tricky enough situation. If your members decide the table is being moved by someone or something outside themselves, it may well become difficult, or even impossible, to achieve voluntary control. This is a limitation when setting out to create a 'Philip' type entity. Also the concept of an unfriendly entity may cause alarm and lead to frightening phenomena. On the other hand, many groups will find it easier to generate phenomena if belief in an independent intelligence is present. Batcheldor sees such an idea as having a strong suggestive effect and also observes that when a group passes control over to a supposed independent intelligence, the group members tend to cease striving to produce phenomena and hence tend to generate better table movements!

With pros and cons on both sides, it seems reasonable to suggest that individual groups must decide for themselves whether they want to achieve voluntary control over the movements or leave things to what may or may not be an independent intelligence. On this point, Batcheldor makes the interesting comment that ordering the table to perform some action is not the same thing as voluntary control. We do not, he says, order our legs to move when we walk – we simply move them. True voluntary control is achieved in the experiments when the group simply moves the table. This is very difficult and requires much practice. A good exercise is to try to make a levitation last longer than usual. You do so by *not* thinking of the table dropping – something easier said than done.

Sooner or later in the course of your experiments, you are likely to find yourself dealing with violent movements – so violent, in fact, that the table itself could actually be smashed.

If these occur during sessions in which an independent intelligence appears to have control, the movements can usually be stopped by removing all hands from the table or switching on the lights. Remember that the entity itself is, quite likely, to be a creation of the group so that if sitters stop being afraid of it and expect it to be more friendly, it will probably quickly become so. During voluntary control sessions, sitters should be instructed to resist the expectation that the table will crash. They should also be assured that if they visualize it stopping on command, then it will stop.

21
Levitations and PK

Conditioning your group to produce PK is a slow, careful process, probably best left to develop at its own pace. Small effects should be attempted, achieved and perfected before you begin to look for the more spectacular phenomena. For this reason, it is probably best to allow your first table levitation to occur spontaneously. But human nature being what it is (and table levitations being something difficult to explain by unconscious muscular action) it is likely that after several successful sessions involving lesser movements, your group will want to try for something more dramatic.

There is, in fact, a procedure you can follow which will, with luck, lead to table levitation phenomena. But before you embark on it, you should be aware of what Batcheldor has whimsically labelled the WOW problem.

WOW stands for 'Will it or won't it?' and is a state of mind arising out of sitter expectations. When something new is about to be attempted, sitters begin to wonder will it or won't it happen? Unfortunately such a state of mind seems to act as a barrier to phenomena and hence should be avoided if at all possible.

Probably the simplest way of avoiding it is not to announce your intentions in advance. Intelligent sitters will, of course, often deduce quite quickly what you are attempting, but a low-key, casual manner can still go a long way towards dampening down WOW.

In order to achieve levitation, begin by ordering the table to perform a series of slides. These need not be particularly dramatic: a foot or so backwards and forwards will do.

Once the slides are well established, order the table to slide and *grow light.*

At this point, if all goes well, you should quickly begin to notice that the slides occur with much less noise than before, as if the table had begun to glide rather than slide. Once this happens, you can instruct the table to 'get light and float up', repeating the command at intervals if necessary. Providing you can avoid the tension of the WOW state, levitation will follow.

It is an irritating fact that not all levitations are easy to detect with certainty, particularly if you are operating in total or near total darkness. This may be a good point to introduce your first piece of test equipment — battery-operated contacts fixed to each leg of the table which will sound a buzzer or light a small bulb if all four feet leave the floor simultaneously.

Levitations, when they occur, will almost certainly be your first example of genuinely paranormal phenomena. But they remain part of the 'hands-on' procedure you adopted from the beginning of your experiments. The next step is to try for table movements without contact with the sitters.

This should, of course, only be attempted after strong movements with contact have been well established over several sittings. There are differing techniques you can use. One is to introduce short (five to ten minute) waiting periods during which spontaneous, no-contact movements may occur. Another is to wait until strong movements with contact are under way, then suggest sitters remove their hands completely and wait for the possibility of further movement. (This is unlikely to occur quickly, incidentally, so be prepared to sit back for anything up to fifteen minutes before deciding the experiment has failed.)

An alternative approach is for sitters to withdraw their hands by stages. After each partial withdrawal, time should be devoted to building up the table movements back to their full strength before any more hands are withdrawn. When the total withdrawal sequence is complete, you should find that movements will continue to occur while the sitters' hands are close to (but definitely clear of) the table.

By the time you reach this stage, you will, in fact, have achieved your goal of inducing genuine gross PK phenomena, although both your sitters and yourself may have some difficulties in believing there is no rational explanation for what is happening. You will wish to introduce tests and controls to validate the phenomena; and chances are you will wish to produce even more spectacular phenomena still.

All this can be done, provided you have patience, move forward gradually and continually bear in mind your greatest enemy is disbelief. But on this last point, we are not simply restating the ancient notion that faith can move mountains (or tables!) but rather presenting a method by which your initial disbelief may be reconditioned by experience.

Batcheldor gives the following synopsis of a successful experimental series, like so much of his work, well worth quoting verbatim:

Start and continue with tasks that seem just plausible in terms of what is already happening. Start with a small, creaky table, not a huge rock-steady one.

Grade the tasks. When the table is going well, put a weight on it; then a larger one. You may then find that you can sit a person on it and tip them off, whereas had you omitted the progressive weights, the table would probably have come to a stop as soon as you put a person on it.

Do not strain credulity by calling for an advanced phenomenon such as levitation too early in the sitting development. Plausibility can be assisted by leaving a loophole for normal explanations, as by working in darkness. Strong light arouses both doubt and emotional resistance so work in darkness at least until phenomena are very well established. Use such rituals as are found to cause the sitters to be expectant.

Pay attention to immobilization of attention by avoiding too much moving about or sensory stimulation. Avoid the kind of conversation that alerts the reasoning faculties. Music, certain kinds of noise, jollity and laughter may all help.

Do not have a gap in which the atmosphere goes cold, particularly when changing from one task to another, harder task.

Do not draw attention to the passage of time, or how much time is left.

Avoid strange surroundings, new sitters or onlookers. Avoid also test conditions because these have an awakening effect on the attention. Arguments come into the same category.

Keep down resistance. This is easier said than done, for resistance cannot be removed except by gradual acclimatization: while still present, it can only be circumvented. Leave loopholes for comfortable explanations, rationalizations and scape-goating until these devices can be done without.

It seems best to optimize rather than minimize tension. It should preferably be a pleasant excitement, not nastily fearful. Both pleasant and fearful tension imply belief and therefore tend to generate an increase in phenomena, but the fearful type carries the danger of generating frightening phenomena. We shape the phenomena with our expectations and beliefs.

Afterword

Nuclear physics took a great leap forward when it was demonstrated that the experimenter could not be divorced from certain experiments. In these experiments, the act of observation became a factor influencing the behaviour of the particles.

Although absolutely accepted today, this discovery was a bombshell in its time since it had been considered a scientific cornerstone that the scientist must (and could) play no part in the phenomena he or she observed.

I believe Kenneth Batcheldor has achieved a fundamentally similar insight in the field of psychical research. For more than a century now, conscientious scientists have attempted to move psi phenomena into the laboratory with, in general, tantalizing, but extremely frustrating results. Anyone involved seriously in this field will confirm the phenomena has an irritating habit of fading away just at the point where it seemed proof positive might be established.

While the search for proof positive has kept scientists busy for the past three or four generations, Batcheldor seems to be among the first to question *why* the phenomena always slips away and to evolve techniques to tackle what he considers the root cause.

His theories make a great deal of sense within the broader context. Anthropologists have long noted that 'magic' seems to work among primitive peoples — with the term 'magic' almost always more properly defined as psychical phenomena. Explanations of this fact have varied from superstition to suggestion, but none have proved particularly useful in any practical sense.

Batcheldor, by contrast, suggests that most — and possibly all — of us have latent psychical abilities. But these are very successfully held in check by our conviction that such abilities are impossible.

It is this very conviction that Batcheldor's methods are designed to undermine.

As we have already seen in the course of the present book, personal convictions, however widely shared by one's peers, may diverge considerably from reality. This is because such convictions are not necessarily based on experience, but arise due to the psychological phenomenon of *conditioning*.

As infants, we are conditioned (taught) to perceive reality in a particular way. The perception ultimately represents the consensus of the society in which we find ourselves; and generally speaking might be considered a good thing. But there will always be aspects of the consensus which are just plain wrong, as the medieval consensus of a flat earth was just plain wrong.

Anyone who has taken the trouble to study the abundant literature on the subject must be convinced there is ample evidence to suggest that psychical powers are a reality. But most of us do not believe it, because we have been strongly conditioned not to believe it.

Our stance is reinforced by personal experience. If PK is possible, why cannot I simply think the book from my library shelf into my hand? Why do I have to rise from my comfortable fireside chair and get it the hard way?

The answer Batcheldor puts forward to these very reasonable questions is that you have been taught to believe thinking the book down is impossible. Thus you never try. Or, if you do try, your own mind, your own belief, prevents the use of your natural PK talents.

This notion is by no means unorthodox (although its specific application is possibly unique). Psychiatric medicine has studied countless cases of hysterical paralysis where physically sound limbs will not move because the patient remains convinced — often at a deeply unconscious level — that they cannot move.

High intelligence is no prophylactic against such unconscious mental gymnastics. There is evidence to suggest that Charles Darwin suffered for many years from a purely hysterical illness.

But given that we recognize the possibility of our minds blocking certain of our natural abilities, we are still faced with the problem of figuring out what to do about it. Intellectual recognition is not enough. The root cause must be tackled and tackled firmly.

Batcheldor's most intriguing insight lies in his use of conditioning to break down conditioning. While his experimental method appears to be directed towards the wooden table in the centre of the room, it is in fact directed towards the sitters around it.

Once this fact is firmly grasped, you will be in a position to structure your own experiments and perhaps go much further than you have ever dreamed.

Index